CHINESE ZODIAC SIGNS

D0808369

CHINESE ZODIAC SIGNS

YEAR OF THE MONKEY

 **1908 · 1920 · 1932
1944 · 1956 · 1968
1980 · 1992 · 2004**

ARROW

Arrow Books Limited
17-21 Conway Street, London W1P 6JD
An imprint of the Hutchinson Publishing Group
London Melbourne Sydney Auckland
Johannesburg and agencies throughout the world
First published by M.A. Editions 1982
Arrow edition 1984
© M.A. Editions 1982

Produced by Aurum Press, 33 Museum Street, London WC1
Original text in French by Catherine Aubier
Translated by Eileen Finletter and Ian Murray
Designed by Julie Francis
Phototypeset in Optima
by York House Typographic, Hanwell, London
Made and printed in Great Britain
by Anchor Brendon Limited, Tiptree, Essex

ISBN 0 09 933500 X

CONTENTS

HOW TO USE THIS BOOK

Each section of this book gives a detailed description of the character, personality and partnership possibilities of the Pig. The characteristics of this sign are described in conjunction with the important ascendant sign.

There is also a synthesis of the Chinese zodiac and the more familiar Western zodiac. Together these give new meaning and depth to the description and prediction of an individual's personality, the main tendencies of his character, his behaviour and the broad outline of his destiny.

The book concludes with the fascinating astrological game, the I Ching.

The arrangement of the book is as follows:
A short introduction to the background and philosophy of the Chinese zodiac (page 8).
A description of the characteristics of your specific Chinese sign, determined by the *year of your birth* — in this case the Monkey (page 19).
The best (and worst) partners for that Sign, determined by *the hour of your birth* (page 43).
The combination and interaction of your sign with the Ascendant Element: Earth, Water, Fire, Wood, Metal (page 52).
The comparison and combination of the two zodiacs — Chinese and Western (for example, the Sagittarian Monkey, the Virgo Monkey) — highlight many subtleties which enable you to clarify your psychological portrait (page 70).
The astrological game of the I Ching, which adapts the ancient Taoist 'Book of Mutations' to each Chinese sign. This simple game offers the reader the opportunity to obtain wise and appropriate answers to abstract as well as everyday questions (page 78).

THE MYSTERIES OF CHINESE ASTROLOGY

中國星相
學之神秘

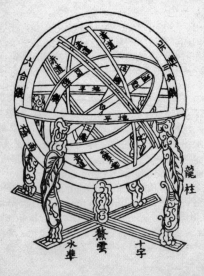

The legend of Buddha

One Chinese New Year more than five centuries before Christ, Buddha invited all the animals in creation to come to him, promising them recompense appropriate to his all-powerful and miraculous kindness and generosity. However, dimmed by their preoccupations of the moment (is it not said in the West that the characteristic of the animal is merely to eat, sleep, couple and fear?), almost all of them ignored the call of the Divine Sage. Yet twelve of the animals did go to him. They were, in order of their arrival, the Rat, Ox, Tiger, Rabbit, Dragon, Snake, Horse, Goat, Monkey, Rooster, Dog and Pig (other traditions replace the Rabbit with the Cat and the Pig with the Wild Boar).

To thank them Buddha offered each a year which would be dedicated to him alone through the ages. This year would carry the animal's name, and express his symbolic character and his specific psychological traits, marking the personality and behaviour of people born during that year.

Thus a cycle of twelve years was established, fitting exactly the sequence and rhythm of this improbable bestiary (one can imagine the dizzying amount of work which would have faced the astrologer if all of the animals had answered Buddha's invitation!).

Such is the legend.

The lunar cycle

Actually, Chinese astrology precedes the development of Far Eastern Buddhism, which began only in the 5th century of the Christian era, or about one thousand years after Buddha's appearance on earth. However, astrologers were already practising their art in China ten centuries before Christ; but the very origins of this astrology are as controversial as they are immemorial.

One point cannot be disputed: contrary to the West, which developed a solar astrology based on the apparent displacements of the daily star as its position in the Western zodiac changed from month to month, the Far East constructed a lunar astrology based on the annual cycle of lunar movements. This is why the Asian New Year — the Tet celebration among the Vietnamese — never falls exactly on the same date (page 94).

While the phases of the moon are equally important for a Western astrologer, their context is inscribed differently, with the result that their play of correspondence — and so their meanings and implications — are not comparable to those of Eastern astrology.

Without entering too deeply into scientific considerations which would lead us away from the purposes of this book, let us simply remind ourselves of the obvious and multiple influences of the moon, for example the movement of the tides, as well as more subtle levels, such as the female cycles and the obscure depths of the psyche. The term 'lunatic' has a precise and, indeed, clinical meaning. Recent statistical studies, for example, have made it possible to establish a strange and significant increase in acts of violence and criminality on nights when there is a full moon. Also, rigorous tests have established the direct impact of the moon on the chemical composition of certain bodies whose molecular structure can be modified depending on whether or not they have been exposed to lunar light.

Nuances of Chinese astrology

So, here we are with our twelve animals, the *Emblems* of Chinese astrology. Does this mean that all persons born in the same year as, say, the Rat or the Horse, will be subject to the same formulae of character and destiny? No more so than that those born under the sign of Aries or Libra are all confined to the same zodiacal script.

In Western astrology, the position of the planets, the calculation of the Ascendant and the Golden Mean of the Sky and its Mansions, allows the astrologer to refine and individualize a given theme considerably. In the same way, in Chinese astrology one obtains some surprisingly detailed and complex results. This is achieved by integrating with the intitial data factors such as the *Companion in Life* (determined by the hour of birth, but not to be confused with the Western Ascendant), and the predominant *Element*, which refers to the five Elements: Earth, Water, Fire, Wood and Metal.

This triple point of view — the *Emblematic Animal*, the *Companion in Life* and the *Element* — provide the reader with a greater diversity of references and a totality of perspectives both more rich and more precise than those found in Western astrology. To this we have added a detailed interpretation of the relationship between the Chinese and Western signs. The two astrologies are by nature distinct but never contradictory, and therefore complementary aspects and fusion can only result in a more profound understanding of the psychological types emanating from them. However, it is important to stress that although the concept of analogy holds an important place in Chinese astrology, it bears neither the same sense nor the same overall significance as in Western astrology.

Each Chinese sign is a universe in itself, a small cosmos with its own laws and domains, completely independent of all other signs. Each of these living creatures is given specific powers and functions, becoming an emblematic animal endowed with a particular dimension peculiar unto itself. It creates its own jungle or cavern, and defines by its rhythm its own cadences and breathing. In this way it secretes its own chemistry — or, rather, its own alchemy. It is a supple, mobile, fluctuating image, governed by its own internal metamorphoses and contradictions.

Once we understand this, we will see that it is fatal to impose a fixed framework or clearly circumscribed area of mental categories and psychological equations in order to protect or reassure an anguished ego seeking a comforting or flattering projection of its own desires and fears.

Our alignment to a Chinese sign cannot be defined by exclusive formulae or linear classifications. The Chinese symbol unfolds slowly, a gift of the Gods, of Time and of Mystery; a delectable or poisoned gift which an Oriental person accepts with humility because he knows that its flavour may be born of the poison, as its poison may be born of the flavour.

Sometimes, in the course of a lifetime, it is circumstances more than a character trait which seem to determine and crystallize the principal tendencies of a sign. In such cases a thread of major or minor events will tend to form a symphonic background to the style of, say, a Dragon or a Rat.

To Have and To Be

Through the centuries Chinese astrology has permeated and inspired the mental attitudes and behaviour of hundreds of millions of people in the Far East, to an extent that is difficult for us to accept or even appreciate.

To understand better the spirit in which these people rely on the art of contemplation in handling the problems of daily life, a cardinal point must be emphasized — one which probably constituted the essential and fundamental difference between Eastern and Western civilizations, and poses a virtually impassable dividing line between them.

In our Western 'consumer society' — irrespective of the admiring or negative feelings we may associate with this expression — the fundamental question, from birth to death and at all levels of activity, is: 'What can I have?'. We are continuously asking what we might possess or enjoy; what material goods, fortune, luck, honours or power might be had; whether we will achieve success in love, prestige, a good job, family, health, home, friends or, on another level, culture and knowledge. It is always a question of, 'What can I obtain, preserve, enlarge?' which underlies the totality of our motivations.

Think of the *models* that are held up to us: the successful politicians, business tycoons, film and stage stars, celebrated artists or scientist, sports champions, heroes of crime novels or comic strips. Idols of all kinds incarnate the triumph and glory of 'to have'. All will say, 'I have the most power, the most money, the most diplomas and abilities', or even, 'Mine is the greatest love affair'. Or, why not 'Mine is the most terrible drama, the most frightful illness'? Esteem is won exclusively from what one *has*.

Still more obvious is advertising, which is omnipresent today, and proclaims that one must absolutely *have* such and such a product in order *to be:* dynamic, seductive, happy, at ease with oneself or wholly fulfilled.

For Orientals, the decisive question is not 'What can I have?' but 'Whom can I be?' The model aspired to is not the great leader, the hero or the champion, but the poor, naked Sage who has attained total freedom and perfect peace within himself. Princes and great businessmen bow low before him, for he is the image of the highest self-realization possible to man. In this perspective, the Sage renounces nothing; on the contrary, since he has attained the supreme reality, he is immeasurably richer than the most powerful ruler.

It is we who, due to our fragmented and illusory attachments, our infantile whims and our incessant conflicts, continually forgo the most marvellous felicity of all — God.

'Who am I?' Whatever approaches and methods, schools, sects or forms of asceticism are followed, this question, in appearance so simple and banal, lies at the base of and is the key to all Oriental culture. Through it lies the way to true liberation, by way of those roads to genuine understanding and knowledge known as Yoga, Vedanta, Tantra, Tao and Zen — to cite only the best known.

All this may cause the Chinese approach to astrology to seem disconcerting to us. The Oriental does not think 'I have such and such predispositions, aptitudes or weaknesses inherent in my horoscope', but rather, 'How can I be a Rat (or a Goat or a Dog) in all the circumstances of my life?'

The Oriental's goal is not 'to have' in the same way in which we in the West say 'I possess such and such a quality or defect'. For him, it is instead a question of directions, implying a subtle and rhythmic progression; a sort of poetic dance of destiny, with each animal possessing its own steps and pirouettes — an entire choreography of its own.

These subtleties must be perceived clearly by those who wish to evolve without losing their way or turning round in circles in this immense domain of shimmering and shifting aspects of understanding.

The astrological I Ching

In the last section of this book, we present a game inspired by the oracles of the I Ching and adapted to each sign.

In his book Zen Buddhism, Alan Watts wrote: 'The I Ching is a work of divination containing oracles based on 64 abstract figures, each composed of six traits. These traits are of two sorts: divided or negative and undivided or positive. A modern psychologist would recognize an analogy with the Rorschach test, whose aim is to establish the mental portrait of an individual according to the spontaneous images suggested to him by an inkspot or an over-elaborate design.

A subject whose images are inspired by the inkspot should be able to use his subsequent perceptions to deduce the necessary practical information to guide his future behaviour. Considered in this way, the divinatory art of the I Ching cannot be attacked as a vulgar superstition.'

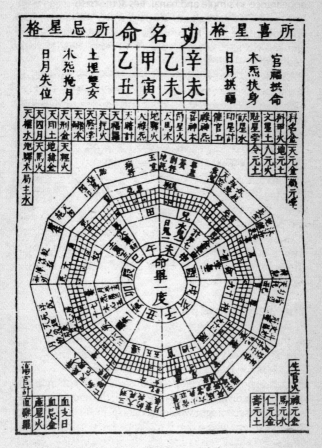

The relationship between the Signs and the Lunar Mansions

The practitioner of the I Ching commands an entire critical survey of the methods available when important decisions have to be made. We, on the other hand, are convinced that our decisions are rational because we depend upon a cluster of valid data affecting a problem; not for us to leave it to a mere game of heads or tails. The practitioner, however, might question whether we know what information is truly valid, given the fact that our plans are being constantly upset by events which are wholly unpredictable. Indeed, if we were rigorously rational in our choices of the data upon which our behaviour depended, so much time would be required that the moment for action would pass before we could assemble the data. Although we may set out initially to seek this information in a scientific manner, we are rapidly forced to act on another basis — capricious intuition, the impossibility of thinking further because we are too exhausted, or simply that time is too short and a choice must be made. In other words, our most important decisions are based largely on impressions, on our capacity to 'feel' a situation.

Every practitioner of the I Ching knows this. He is aware that his method is not an exact science but a useful and effective approach, if he is endowed with sufficient powers of intuition or, as he would say, *in the Tao*.

THE YIN AND THE YANG

The *Yin* and the *Yang* are the symbols of two opposing and complementary principles whose indissoluble play and constant metamorphosis represent the roots, indeed the very tissues of the universe in action. They represent the eternal opposites — Positive-Negative, Yes-No, White-Black, Day-Night, Full-Empty, Active-Passive, Masculine-Feminine, and so on. Each contains within itself the germ of the other. That is why the man (Yang) bears within himself a feminine component (Yin), and the woman (Yin) a masculine one (Yang).

The Yin-Yang coupling is both indissoluble and changeable, each of the two terms being also its opposite and complementary term. This is expressed by the traditional figure:

At the moment when the Yang (white, active) is at its apogee — the bulging, enlarged part — the Yin (black, passive) imperceptibly takes its place — the tapering part — and vice verse.

The Yin and the Yang have no 'moral' character, neither is superior nor inferior to the other. Their antithesis is as necessary and as little in conflict as that of the left hand and the right hand striking together to applaud.

THE YIN AND THE YANG TYPES

The Rat, Ox, Rabbit, Monkey, Dog and Pig are **Yin**.
The Tiger, Horse, Dragon, Snake, Goat and Rooster are **Yang**.

The Yin man

Appearance: The Yin man is often corpulent, of medium height and muscularly well developed. He is physically resilient to a marked degree and his health is sound. He often has a round face and does not smile much.

Psychology: The Yin man is above all self-preoccupied and inclined to consider himself the centre of the universe. Though his behaviour appears calm, his moods are unstable and susceptible to his immediate environment. He has great confidence in himself, yet fears failure. Sociable, hospitable, he is optimistic vis-à-vis himself and others. His life is active; he is pragmatic and efficient.

The Yang man

Appearance: He is of average weight, often tall and slender, even willowy. His face is smiling and he prefers strong colours. Of delicate health, he should be advised to prevent rather than wait to cure illness.

Psychology: The Yang man is an individualist and attracted to introspective meditation. He is intelligent, independent and at times solitary. He prefers his own company and communing with nature to living with the crowd. Contrary to the Yin man, he seeks his equilibrium within himself instead of finding it amongst others.

THE DOMAINS
OF
THE MONKEY

十二生肖

THE MONKEY AND ITS SYMBOLISM

'The Monkey is considered by some as both Yin and Yang. It is the symbol of intelligence and a sometimes slightly dishonest ingenuity. Does not the Monkey-God owe his immortality to the peach that he stole in the garden of the Sovereign Mother of the West? His life-span is several thousand years. From his youth until eight hundred years, he is not always benevolent, but he improves with age, and, when he is transformed into a baboon, he becomes charming and helpful.'

'Sharp as a monkey' is a common expression, but the term 'crafty' fits the monkey better. Crafty, agile, clownish, the monkey is a disconcerting animal which continues to surprise us, to baffle us. Leaping from branch to branch, he symbolizes the consciousness of the palpable world. 'The mastery of the Monkey' is that of the heart; it is thus that he is described in certain methods of Buddhist meditation, expressing a control of perpetually roving emotions. In the beautiful Chinese book of the *Si-yeou-KI*, the Monkey is designated as 'Son of Sky and of Earth'. In India he is found as the extremely adroit, spontaneous, agile and whimsical monkey called Hanumänn. This personage represents the perfect servant of God, the perfect adorer. 'He disposes of immense strength. But he does not use this power for egotistical ends, for the satisfaction of his own desires, for his own glory, but puts it entirely at the service of his master, his God, and attributes to himself no merit.'

In Asia the Monkey is also synonymous with wind — the West wind. Like the wind, he suddenly rises up, gambols, flies away and disappears with one bound. Is he white or is he black? Is he Yin or is he Yang? He is both, this magician, this acrobat. He is intelligent and ambiguous and master of the instinctive and creative forces that he liberates. He roves his universe and the irrational, jumping about on the spokes of the Wheel of Time. He is the tightrope walker, vigilant and superciliously bantering; for ever on the lookout for the fall of his fellow creatures. At times indifferent to notions of good and evil, but perfectly lucid, he is a wily confederate, ready to disappear at a moment's notice, carrying off the stolen fruit.

But let us return to the Monkey of the *Si-yeou-KI*.

In China, within the border of the eastern regions, the Monkey was a rock which, since the beginning of the world, received the rays of the moon and of the sun. One day the rock swelled and burst, giving birth to a stone egg. A hurricane broke, the egg split, and from it emerged a stone monkey. He possessed all five senses: sight, hearing, smell, taste and touch. After much training, he succeeded in travelling to the North, South, East and West, nourishing himself on the fruits of the trees and the water of the rivers. Later, he lived in the mountains, sleeping at night on the lower slopes and climbing to the summits during the daytime. In this way he became friendly with other monkeys, the gibbons.

One very hot day, the Monkey, accompanied by the gibbons, went into a little wood of pine trees, in the middle of which bubbled a deep and cool stream. At the sight of such pure, sparkling water, they decided to plunge in to find its source and measure its depth. The Monkey's companions agreed to proclaim King whoever could descend to the bottom of the stream. The stone monkey dived in first. Having arrived at the bottom, he opened his eyes. He discovered not water but a large palace on which was engraved, 'Mount of flowers and of fruits, land of happiness, celestial cavern'.

The Monkey hurried back to the surface to tell the gibbons what he had discovered. The gibbons were happy and danced with joy. Then the stone monkey said to them 'We are going to live in the palace. We will be sheltered from the sun and the rain.' All the monkeys then plunged into the water and took possession of the Palace of Happiness. The stone monkey installed himself on a seat and had himself proclaimed King, as had been agreed. He was named Perfect Monkey-King.

However, despite his glory as a sovereign, laden with riches and power, the Perfect Monkey-King was melancholy: he feared old age and death.

One day, he decided to leave the Palace to search for immortality. Riding on the wind, he looked in the furthest reaches of caverns and in the azure of the sky. In the course of his quest, the Monkey's body and spirit little by little changed completely, and he ended by becoming a man.

This tale nicely illustrates a typical Oriental idea: intelligence, courage, prestige, fortune and power — all are worthless unless the fundamental mysteries of life and death are studied and understood thoroughly.

A few notes on the Monkey

Principal qualities: Intelligence, clear-sightedness, keenness of mind.

Principal defects: A slight superiority complex and often indulges in a low opinion of others.

Work: Able, ambitious, gifted in everything, the Monkey's powers are far-ranging. All doors are open to him.

Best role: A gentleman-thief such as Raffles.

Worst role: He has none because he can be the best around, so long as he wants to be.

Money: Rich from time to time — due to luck or cleverness — but too spendthrift to remain so for long.

Luck: He is the animal most adapted to life on earth; and if he is born in summer, his luck will be all the greater.

Cannot live without: Movement, discussion, the exchanging of ideas.

Adores: Taking care of others, for he has a feeling for chivalry.

Detests: Feeling excluded, ignored or another's indifference and, above all, for his self-confidence to be shaken.

Leisure activities: He is sociable and likes to circulate. He loves social meetings, cocktails, smart parties, and, above all, to be adulated.

Favourite places: Everywhere, provided life is intense and he is not bored; he enjoys being on holiday, and even his office, if he likes his work.

Colour: Violet.

Plants: Sandalwood and cedarwood.

Flower: Elderberry.

Professions: Politician, diplomat, ambassador, writer, spokesman, storyteller, orator, salesman, actor — and thief.

The four ages in the life of the Monkey, according to Chinese tradition

The infancy of the Monkey will be happy and without problems: he is intelligent, hard-working and adapts easily. His *youth*, however, will be unstable, full of changes and emotional difficulties. In *maturity*, the Monkey will achieve some tranquillity and success — but watch out for *old age* when he will often be solitary and cut off from family and loved ones.

THE PSYCHOLOGY OF THE MONKEY

For the layman, Chinese astrology poses a problem similar to that found in Western astrology: that of dividing humanity into twelve different psychological types. We are imbued with a sense of our individuality, our tastes, our times and of our culture — and we cling to these sacrosanct distinctions. It is sometimes difficult to admit that our neighbour upstairs, that insupportable creature, has the nerve to share a sign of the zodiac with us, be it Oriental or Occidental. How much more comforting it would be to relegate what we pompously call the 'dregs of humanity' to a thirteenth undetermined sign, a depository of our rancours and our prejudices.

Given that there is no such 'sign' in astrology, some of the people we encounter have inherited unfortunate, and not always justified, reputations. In Western astrology, the signs of Virgo and Scorpio have attracted many unflattering epithets; the same occurs in Oriental astrology, and the Monkey is one such zodiacal 'scapegoat'.

Tradition accords him with an expansive and magnanimous nature, the greatest intelligence and the keenest lucidity. Equally, it also dispenses a litany of faults with which to categorize him: he is a liar, garrulous, hypocritical and unstable.

Being interested in Chinese astrology, I have never been able to resist the temptation to seek out among my circle of friends and acquaintances the influence of certain signs and psychological or other constants which they are supposed to express. These little studies have resulted in a high percentage of statistical accuracy. There was, however, one exception: of the twelve signs of the Chinese zodiac, only the Monkey remained obscure and apparently remote from his human counterparts. In an attempt to establish what they had in common, I closely observed and listened to my friends born under his sign, and studied long lists of celebrities born in his year. This proved difficult and often inconclusive, and I have the distinct impression that those born under the sign of the Monkey must feel ill-at-ease in reading about some of the character traits ascribed to them.

Evidently, there is a lack of agreement between the moving, complex reality of the 'nature' of the sign and the slightly arbitrary simplicity of the texts describing it. One then asks why this is. For one reason, classic Chinese astrological literature seems to judge those born under the sign of the Monkey on their *appearance* (the same is true, though less so, for those born under the sign of the Rooster). This is misleading. Monkeys are indeed jokesters, actors and manipulators of ideas; but they do not always behave so either on purpose or with bad intentions. They are accused of wishing to dominate others, to decide everything for them, and of having a frightening superiority complex. This is true. But one forgets that, due to their superior intellectual capacities, they naturally tend to dominate others, and that they frequently make wise decisions which many would do well to imitate.

In fact, Monkeys are indeed special. The best adapted to the world we live in, they are the most likely to get the best out of it. No wonder they provoke jealousy and misunderstanding.

Among the Monkeys I know personally, I have noticed some common characteristics: they share an entirely unique blend of vivacity, fantasy and detachment. In a matter of minutes, one acquaintance of mine will change from a joyous, playful, devil-may-care person to a haughty and responsible intellectual; all done with a slight, secretive and ironic smile.

Another close friend will burst out with a stream of ideas so disorganized and irrational that he would dazzle any psychoanalyst — and then return to his office to manage his little world with an iron hand.

Monkeys also share a natural facility for expressing themselves in a clear, precise and convincing manner. Their behaviour is professional, efficient and responsible. They are remarkably adaptable and show a young, fresh and enthusiastic side that is ready to embark on any crusade to seek the Holy Grail, the unknown or the unprecedented. Monkeys hate regularity and abhor routine and repetitive tasks. When they are solicited, even hustled, the adrenalin flows and they find the incentive to use their ingenuity and their capacity to make swift decisions. Outsiders do not easily understand this facility. It is so disconcerting; is there *nothing* they cannot do?

Monkeys are independent, swift people with particularly lively minds and a gift for repartee, but they sometimes lack perseverance and concentration. Liking variety and change, they will find concentrating on a single problem desperately boring. They easily spread their interests far and wide among a wide variety of things, and show an infinite curiosity about anything and everything. Their thirst for knowledge is unquenchable. They actually do know a great deal, but their impulsive, lighthearted manner disguises this and consequently they are considered to be more superficial than they really are.

Their gregarious nature, the ease with which they sidestep the problems of others, does not cause people to feel indulgent towards them.

It is here that we find the real secret, the true drama of those born under the sign of the Monkey: by flitting about, criticizing, propounding and dominating, they bring about reproaches and are misunderstood. One might think that they do not care, for they always lightly evade the issue even, if necessary, cruelly mocking themselves. They have, in fact, a great sense of humour and rarely take themselves seriously. In truth they may suffer profoundly from this feeling of exclusion, becoming pessimistic, bitter and sceptical, but without revealing a hint of these feelings to others.

Monkeys wish to be admired, loved with indulgence and affection and understood. But they hardly even confide in others, opening out to them and revealing their true nature. They seem to need to evade understanding. It is difficult to know whom or what they are defending.

So, never hesitate to hold out your hand when you see a Monkey somersaulting on the flying trapeze of his fantasy; perhaps, waiting only for that, he will in turn lay his head on your shoulder.

The Monkey has a generous nature; he wants to be chivalrous. He takes great care of others, is tactful, adroit and sensitive. But he is also too rational and, finding it difficult to put himself in the place of others, regrets this bar to his comprehension, for at bottom he is always reasonable.

With friends, he cannot keep quiet. He loves to talk about himself and them. In dialogue he blossoms: the exchange enhances! He is forceful rather than violent; his crown sits on a world of language and of literature, not of war.

He may seem unfeeling, but that is a misconception. Quite simply, he cannot prevent himself from filtering his emotions and feelings through an intelligence as agile as his gestures. He is both a child and an old man. Deep within him the two carry on an interminable dialogue, the old man throwing cold water on the child, the child rejecting the pessimism of the old man. The Monkey, always ironically self-absorbed, is highly personal, different and original — even when he tries to agree with everyone. Even in moments of great sociability, he will find it difficult to avoid throwing out an accurate and rather cutting remark about the personal characteristics of the person facing him. He has, in fact, observation as sharp as a laser beam.

THE MONKEY AS A CHILD

Here is one of the easiest of children to educate — at least Chinese tradition believes so. If you are worried about potential problems, bear a Monkey child.

The young Monkey is 'easy' to raise because learning is not difficult for him. Intelligent, gifted, brilliant, sociable, he adapts marvellously to school life; in particular, he often has a gift for languages.

If he returns home from school to a horrible slum where an alcoholic father beats him regularly, and a schizophrenic mother and a tubercular little sister await him, he will still have an excellent chance of surviving without traumas. Where, for example, a young Dog would be marked for life and would attempt to hide the shameful defects of his family, the Monkey will write a play or a novel about his unhappy childhood. Dickens was a Monkey.

If unhappy with his family, our young Monkey will quickly find others — intellectuals or athletes — and join their communities and clubs; he does not lack imagination.

To keep a hold on him, you must above all interest him. He needs dialogue and surprises; he likes to share your problems and your occupations. I have a Monkey girlfriend who speaks tenderly about the years of her childhood when she assisted her busy midwife mother. Perhaps a mother who had worked quietly in a dull office would have filled her with less admiration.

With this kind of child, the parents' role consists above all in gently curbing an accelerated mental development. They must encourage their little Monkey to wait for others, to put himself in their place, to be less ironic — or at least to learn the difference between an amusing joke and a hurtful criticism. That is about all. Oh, no, I almost forgot — they must also reread their Classics if they are to keep up with a child who learns and assimilates with remarkable facility.

LOVE LIFE

Among the Monkeys whom I know, all have acquired an honourable, even exceptional, success in their professions. All have a rather lively social life and are surrounded by friends. But — all are also alone, or are on the point of becoming so, or have just become so. The Monkey is too rational for his love life to be an easy one. Excepting, naturally, the first moments of passion and enthusiasm, the intoxication of doing everything together, they rarely remain in a state of loving bliss for more than a few months. Sometimes, because of their intelligence and clarity of mind, without meaning to, Monkeys will quickly sense in their loved one the slightest slackening of tension or interest. This will undermine their self-confidence and provoke them into running away to protect the most intimate recesses of their psyches. Usually, it is the Monkeys who give up; they are too aware of the minute detail that is amiss. It is well known that love, if it is to last, must be touched by blindness, and that the most difficult moment is when one discovers the faults of the other. For those born under the sign of the Monkey, this is as hard to weather as Scylla and Charybidis combined. The strength of their attachment is not strong enough for them to resist the stark landscape that their pitiless eyes and their sharp lucidity reveal. I know one female Monkey who is profoundly taken with a gentleman whom she cannot refrain from criticizing. I know another who cannot find her soul-mate, because she quickly discovers 'the point on which we could never get along'. In fact, if Monkeys ever have a really marvellous memory of a liaison, it is usually because it was impossible anyway, or quickly curtailed by absence. In such circumstances they can remain very much in love.

These animals always behave with great charm and kindness, for they love to please and vaguely fear that they will not be liked. They are easily carried away, seducing you with a flick of the wrist and throwing themselves with intensity into each new love. But be careful: it is temptation and conquest they adore. Otherwise, they will follow instantly the first member of the opposite sex who passes by.

FAMILY LIFE

Those born under the sign of the Monkey often marry young, when their passions are fully aflame and their reason is inhibited. Later, they come to a different point of view because their reasonableness causes them to look without illusion upon the romantic world of fairy-tale love which has led other signs to divorce or estrangement. Marvellously adapted to reality, Monkeys know how to be content with it; it is rare to see them drop the substance for the shadow. If they are told that 'the grass is always greener. . .', they will not budge without first getting a sample and an analysis of the terrain. These Monkeys are not crazy. . . .

By nature Monkeys are not faithful, but they can become so, naturally. The family is neither their end nor be all, nor their universal panacea; but once there, they decide, why run elsewhere? And do not, unless certain that something better is to be found.

And then, Monkeys adore children. They themselves are the most eternally young of all the Chinese zodiac, and neither the lines on their faces nor worldly experience will deprive them of that eternal 'youthfulness of spirit' which is their principal charm. It is not naivety nor romanticism, but simply an unfailing resilience which makes them always ready to begin again. For their children, who find themselves at once carried away, stimulated and understood, this enthusiasm is wonderfully enlivening. The Monkey parent always has an indulgent and complicitous eye, for he is aware, despite his children's most colossal blunders and their most catastrophic stupidities, of his own capacity to do worse. Do not expect rigorous lectures nor moralizing from him: he would not last five minutes without laughing. But he has no equal when it comes to sharing in the games, reading and the work of his children — all done with total sincerity.

For varying reasons, children of the Ox or the Dog will adapt badly to a Monkey parent: they either need disciplining or moral protection; precautions that are totally foreign to the Monkey. Such children will be unhappy and dissatisfied. On the other hand, Goat, Rabbit, Tiger, Snake, Pig, Dragon and Horse children — and Monkey children too — will learn a lot from the tricks of their Monkey parent. The little Rat, as well as the young Rooster, will do everything they can to follow, but their Monkey parent will not always reciprocate the intense, blind love they bring and dream of receiving in return.

PROFESSIONAL LIFE

Those born under the sign of the Monkey are independent, crafty and ambitious. Although they clearly prefer to succeed on their own without owing anything to anyone, they are capable of assessing how to profit from the goodwill of those around them, or from the assistance that a relative or a friend in the 'right place' can give them. Diversity is a spur, and they hate tasks that are too routine, preferring situations requiring ingenuity and resourcefulness. When the unexpected fails to occur, they prove capable of inventing it, either by sowing disorder and discord among their professional colleagues (at worst), or by inventing original and distracting hobbies. In the latter case they do their daily job with diligence and vivacity — while thinking of everything they are going to be able to do once the day's work is done.

Monkeys have a speciality in which they are champions: they always occupy their time to the full; not a minute is wasted. Where Snakes or Rabbits spend hours asking themselves vaguely what there is to do, Monkeys will finish off their eight-hour working day by going to the gym or the swimming pool, getting out their accounts or reading a story to their children — in between which they will have started the washing machine, fed the pets and turned on the iron. They are unequalled in their ability to do thirty-six things at once, while being perfectly relaxed and efficient.

This virtuosity brings excellent results in their professional life. Intelligent and gifted with an almost perfect memory and a remarkable facility for adaptation, Monkeys are capable of anything — in the best sense fo the word. No avenue is closed to them — it is enough that they wish to arrive. They will, however, be more at ease in professions requiring contacts, movement and communication; in any case where solutions must be worked out and utilized. They are excellent intermediaries. Supple and opportunistic, they are also decision-makers and will not hesitate to shake up everyone if their business seems to be succumbing to routine. They love to be in the forefront, responsible only to themselves, free; in short, to move around as they please.

MATERIAL LIFE

Monkeys are not noted for their altruism. It is rare to run into them at a charity event — unless they have a personal fortune or need to display a flattering, philanthropic image of themselves. They are preoccupied with profitability, comfort, love and the independence that money can buy. They are quite capable of asking for a loan when they are broke. They are generous only to their families, especially their children, for whom they stop at nothing and would plunder Eldorado to give them Christmas presents. But the rest of the time they prefer to spend money on their own pleasure.

Mr Monkey likes to play lord of the manor. As for Mrs Monkey, it is inadvisable — unless you wish to face immediate ruin — to open an unlimited credit account for her at a large department store. She is capable of spending a month's salary on eccentric trifles that she will wear once and then give to her maid; the next day she will go to her boss and charm him into giving her an advance on her salary. Monkeys are improvident in this way.

However, their ingenuity usually suffices to get them out of the most difficult corners: it is always at the moment when you believe them to be on the point of going to prison for debt that you see their photograph in a newspaper, shaking the hand of Mr Rockefeller and concluding a particularly fruitful and juicy deal. You simply never can tell about Monkeys.

Their spendthrift and carefree side often coexists with great financial ability. This is, to say the least, surprising: they are as ready to administer and multiply their money as they are to throw it out of the window. However that may be, in their material life there is a guiding thread: they cannot bear to deprive themselves, and they never fail to buy pretty and original things. In any case, they are too skilful to go bankrupt. If one day you recognize sprawled in the back seat of a gold Rolls-Royce the person you have seen many mornings begging in front of the bus stop, you can be sure that he is a Monkey.

ENVIRONMENT

Although not slaves of their environment, nor passionately attached to places and objects belonging to their childhood, Monkeys are refined and have good tastes. They enjoy decorating, repainting and moving house; and, when they do not travel with their own furniture and objects, it amuses them to change their surroundings with original and varied accessories: a pagoda or possibly some 16th century French object. Their favourite environment embodies variety: they would adore a flat with walls made of movie screens on which to project different landscapes each day, changing the colours as they wished. Male or female, they are generally remarkable handymen, often with a touch of genius. They are also willing helpers: whenever I have to use a hammer or a drill, I call on my Monkey friends for help — an immediate solution is guaranteed. The toolbox holds no secrets for them; they know how to do everything, from fitting bookshelves to putting up a partition, hanging tapestries or framing a picture.

However, when it comes to tidying up, it is better to put them in an armchair with a glass, lest you find the sausages in your makeup kit and your socks in the fridge. Their wardrobes are always filled to bursting with clothes and forgotten papers, all piled with joyous abandon. Once every ten years they will clear everything out in order to choose what to keep, and will burst out laughing or become sentimental over their incredible mountain of possessions — mementoes of their rich, full life.

A guide to personal relations with a Monkey
Methods of seduction:
He: Before your dazzled eyes, he holds out bright prospects of a fascinating future, rich in the unexpected and the exciting. He makes you drunk on his words and gestures and persuades you that your life with him will be different (which is absolutely true!).

She: Carries on an intelligent conversation and gives you the impression that you are the most brilliant individual ever born. She does this vivaciously and radiantly, and, in truth, with just a little provocation.

If he loves you: He will do everything he can to seduce you, even if it involves kidnapping you, renting a plane or setting fire to your house so that he may be your shining knight. There are two possible solutions: flee or give in, depending on whether or not you have a taste for risk.

He expects of you: That you are always available and that you need him.

To keep you: He is the best armed of the Chinese zodiac and, if he truly wishes, he will transform your life into such a giddy whirl that, without realizing it, you will wake up one day to your golden wedding anniversary.

If he is unfaithful: It is only for pleasure, because he wants to. Do not try to be moralistic — unless you want to hear that if you were more amusing he would not want to.

If you are unfaithful: Beware; this is a dangerous game. Though neither exclusive nor jealous, the Monkey hates to be made a fool of. He is capable of Machiavellian vengeance and it is you, in the end, who will often appear ridiculous. Equally, it is useless to try to hide anything; he is so observant, so astute, that he will scent the danger before you are even aware of it.

In case of a break between you: Try to remain friends; it is worth it. You will succeed in this if you avoid emotional blackmail and jealous scenes.

If you wish to give him a gift: Give him something to be transformed — from a piece of cloth to make a dress with to an old hut overrun with weeds. With a single wave of his magic wand he will create a fashionable gown or a lovely country cottage. Never hesitate to appeal to his resourcefulness and his imagination.

If you want to seduce him: Take him to the airport and buy a ticket for the first flight out. (You will buy the necessary clothes when you get there.)

If you want him to leave: Tell him, preferably in public, 'Oh no, not that one again, you have told it so many times!'

THE MONKEY AND THE OTHER CHINESE SIGNS

Monkey/Rat

It is difficult in the case of a Monkey/Rat relationship to advise that they should avoid each other like the Plague. If you did, they would escape many difficult problems and complications; but it is precisely complications that they love, along with the risk that the relationship is likely to be somewhat tortuous.

Alike on many levels, the Rat and the Monkey are capable of being accomplices and can enjoy themselves together. But one will always be trying to get the better of the other, to dominate without seeming to do so. Each will say in turn, 'I am stronger; I got him that time.' But they will both be mistaken.

If they are friends or associates, their alliance will be unstable but dynamic. If they are in love, their situation becomes more critical, for the rational Monkey is incapable of following the Rat into the depths of his passion or of paying him the attention he requires. When it suits him, the Monkey will be variously charming, attentive and considerate, intoxicating his Rat with flowery phrases; then he will turn cold, indifferent and inconsiderate. This can shatter the Rat, who must take care, for his equilibrium is in danger, and the Monkey will dominate him too often for comfort.

Monkey/Ox

The Ox will understandably be left nonplussed and dizzy by the Monkey's vivacity. But it will not be long before he overcomes his natural distrust and comes to admire those famous pirouettes of his partner; for the Monkey fulfils his own need for originality.

For his part, the lucid Monkey appreciates to a fine degree the Ox's stability and native equilibrium, for these provide the security necessary for one whose centre of gravity constantly oscillates.

Also important is the fact that these two signs are perhaps the least 'sentimental' of the Chinese Zodiac. They do not give love priority in their lives. Each will welcome a partner for whom jealous scenes, emotional displays and 'stupid' declarations of love are foreign. This will be a sound alliance, both in marriage and in business. In the case of the latter, they will, moreover, be formidable allies, but it will be unwise to rely on them when you are the one in difficulty, because compassion is not their strong point.

Monkey/Tiger

Despite his adventurous side, the Tiger is much less supple and adaptable than the Monkey. While respecting his partner's freedom, he likes clear-cut situations: 'What do you mean? Are you with me or with him? You must choose whom you want!' But the Monkey, even when really in love, has too great a desire to please, to measure the effects of his charm and to remain steadily in place to maintain the Tiger's preconceived and fixed role of him. He will always escape from the Tiger, who will be outraged at being walked over like a rug.

Then too, the Monkey mocks, criticizes and is adept at putting his finger on the weak points of those close to him. He will secretly admire the Tiger, but he will not be able to stop himself from tweaking his moustache. Tradition has it that the vexed Tiger will then wait for the Monkey to fall asleep in order to devour him.

However, with much love on the part of the Monkey, and much moderation and tolerance on the part of the Tiger, the relationship can work.

Monkey/Rabbit

The intelligent and wily Monkey knows very well how to manage his affairs, but from time to time he enjoys finding understanding and rest with the indulgent and discreet Rabbit. The Rabbit knows all about wiliness, using it himself to get out of many a difficult situation. The Monkey's advice will enable the Rabbit to add several strings to his bow by making him more reasonable.

These two can attain a form of intimacy and complicity which is extremely personal and from which most people will feel excluded. Moreover, they will be so interested in each other that they will barely wish to raise a large family.

In business their understanding can be ticklish because the Rabbit, who is strongly attached to principles, will be scandalized by the occasional nearly illegal convolutions of the Monkey. He will criticize him, even though at bottom he envies him, and the Monkey will make fun of the Rabbit and disregard his virtuous indignation.

Monkey/Dragon

Avoid this couple if you value the company of those versed in philosophical inquiry. Such pursuits are not their strong point; in fact, both have a tendency to believe that they have delved deeply into a subject when a great deal remains yet to be explored.

They are helped as a couple because each stops at the same point of inquiry, which they will later resume. The Monkey has all the qualities necessary to seduce a Dragon and to keep a hold on him — a rare talent. Knowing how to listen, and then, with a toss of the head, to steal away; to alternate enthusiastic compliments with courteous silences, the Monkey will fascinate the Dragon. The latter, with his unselfish, chimerical and gratuitous side, will know how to captivate the Monkey, who is always seeking a new source of excitement. There will be no rivalry between them; on the contrary, they will complement each other and give each other confidence. Their combination will enable mutual success and other poor mortals, stunned by their charm, will be easily seduced. If a Dog, for example, tries to denounce them as being superficial, they will not hear him.

Monkey/Snake

With this couple there will be excellent intellectual under-standing because, on this level, they are the most 'endowed' of the Chinese zodiac. Both assimilate easily, think quickly and effortlessly and adapt themselves to just about every-thing.

They complete each other: the Monkey is cleverer on the surface, the snake in depth. They make an excellent profes-sional team — unbeatable and crammed with ideas and pos-sibilities — and should not hesitate to become associates.

Emotionally, it is another story. The Monkey is traditionally one of the rare signs capable of eluding the Snake's grasp. He will not allow himself to be eaten and the Snake, disgusted, will not persevere for very long and will look for more acquiescent prey. Their reciprocal fidelity will not last for long.

They should remain friends — something easier to attain, and more profitable.

Monkey/Horse

There is difficult understanding between these two; one is dominated by emotion, living his passions with intensity and with total, ardent commitment; the other, subject to reason, is always conscious of the traps along the way, of the risks of love, and is forever 'standing back' and doubting the possibility of a lasting attachment.

The sincerity of the Horse might help the Monkey to attain some stability, but the latter will attribute this sincerity to naivety or blindness. On his side, the Horse will not stand for the about-faces of the Monkey, and will accuse him of being calculating or insensitive. They will both be wrong, but that will not alter things.

In any case, this couple is rare because the Horse and the Monkey are not often attracted to each other. Even at first sight, when they do not yet know each other, they share a vague distrust, each suspecting the other of superficiality.

Monkey/Goat

This is a relationship full of gaiety and fantasy. These two will never be bored together and will be very amusing for others, ceaselessly inventing new pranks and using their imagination and intelligence with remarkable virtuosity. They will know how to make the most of each other, tossing the ball back and forth.

In fact, everything will go well so long as they remain friends or associates — or even lovers. However, if they decide to live together they will run the risk of things becoming less rosy and idyllic.

In spite of himself, the Monkey will preserve his reasonableness, whereas the Goat will need to be told over and over again that he is loved, so that he may feel truly cared for and secure.

Once the initial enthusiasm has passed, the Goat will be disappointed; the Monkey, even with the best intentions in the world, will not be able to become what he is not — not even to please the Goat.

Monkey/Monkey

Relationships between persons who resemble each other are often advised against or criticized; though interesting and easy, only rarely are they constructive and capable of development. Here, however, is the exception to the rule, for those born under the sign of the Monkey are too clear-sighted and too intelligent to set themselves up as rivals. On the contrary, this relationship enables them to become even more intelligent and efficient — and above all, close accomplices. Understanding each other without effort, each encouraging and stimulating the other, our two Monkeys will go far and will have a marvellous time together.

Naturally, it would be best if they shared some intellectual or material goal. Mad passion will not interest them forever, and they will need something else to bind them as time passes. Since neither of them will make particularly passionate demands on the other, the relationship should work.

Monkey/Rooster

This alliance can work, but only superficially. While the astute, clever Monkey and the honest, frank Rooster complete each other, the former will always have a tendency to mock, criticize and treat the Rooster as a superficial, naive person. The Rooster, on the other hand, will for a while admire the acrobatic games of his partner, but will end by saying: 'Ah, I didn't realize that he was so superficial!'

By judging each other solely on external appearances, they will methodically detect the mote in their companion's eye and not the dust in their own.

Their problem is that they cannot accept that they are on an equal footing, and so they live at war with each other as perpetual rivals. However, a little indulgence and acceptance of the other 'as he is', without wishing to change him, would enable this couple to live in comparative peace.

They can agree on one level: their mutual taste for parties and social life. They will squabble ceaselessly, but what a handsome couple they make!

Monkey/Dog

These two both have a tendency to criticize and are slightly cynical; they have few illusions about their neighbours and voluntarily cultivate the bitter flowers of irony. But there is a snag: the Dog is profoundly idealistic; he is the kind to shout 'All is lost save honour!' and similar, which will seem completely unrealistic to a Monkey, who is more of an opportunist and not at all altruistic.

Between a Dog child and a Monkey parent, between childhood friends or between a brother and sister who have grown up together, a relationship would be possible. But as a couple? The Dog will be profoundly disappointed but will not dare to say so. Little by little he will build up an enormous amount of resentment, being jealous of the Monkey's carefree attitude and, indeed, of his lack of scruples. He will harbour this resentment, feeling that the Monkey is quite disgraceful, but that his tricks work for him, and unjustly so.

As for the Monkey, he will quickly become bored, and make off. Deep down, he is too uneasy to accommodate another's misgivings.

Monkey/Pig

The Pig is perhaps the only sign capable of disarming the manipulative instincts of the Monkey, who will remain mesmerized and admiring in the face of such loyal, indeed royal, honesty. What is this bizarre animal who gives himself without expecting anything in exchange; and who, in his very guts, believes in a good and charitable humanity? Is he a madman, or is he a wise man modestly imbued with the Truth?

The Monkey will find himself caught up in this relationship before having had the time to ask such questions. Though good at seeing through the underhandness of his adversaries, the Monkey is flabbergasted by genuine frankness and generosity. He will do no harm to the Pig, and, seeing himself reflected in such a positive fashion in his partner's eyes, he will believe himself to be a better person — and will become so.

The Pig will rub his hands and laugh in his beard. He knew perfectly well that he would have the last word: his apparent naivety hides a cleverness and abilities far superior to that of the Monkey, simply because he is not in the least bit self-seeking.

SOME MONKEY CELEBRITIES

Byron, Julius Caesar, Chamberlain, Captain Cook, Couperin, Descartes, Diaghilev, Dickens, Dos Passos, The Dumas, Fellini, El Greco, Lyndon Johnson, Buster Keaton, Jack London, Milton, Modigliani, Paderewski, Bertrand Russell, de Sade, Scaramouche, Schopenhauer, Elizabeth Taylor, Spinoza, Chekov, Truman, Leonardo da Vinci.

YOUR
COMPANION
IN LIFE

生命伴侶

After the Chinese sign of your year of birth, here is the sign of your hour of birth

What is a Companion in Life, as understood in Chinese astrology? It is a sort of 'ascendant' sign corresponding to your hour of birth. This Companion is another animal belonging to the Chinese cycle of the twelve emblematic beasts, who falls into step with you and accompanies you, ever ready to help you brave the traps and ambushes along your route. A permanent and benevolent shadow, he can render the impossible possible.

He is your counterpart, but with his own character and tendencies and with a different psychology. Both guardian angel and devil's advocate, he will be a witness to your life and an actor in it.

Have you ever felt, deep inside yourself, the subtle presence of another 'myself' inhabiting you and with whom you live, at times in harmony, at others in conflict? Another self who sometimes criticizes you and at others encourages you? That is your Companion in Life.

There are times when he will appear to be an imposter or an intruder. Certainly, he often questions your habits and your moral or spiritual complacency. Accompanied by this companion, a shadow within, the route is less monotonous and the voyager multiplies his chances of arriving at his chosen destination. This, however, in itself matters little, for it is the journey and the manner in which it is conducted that are important. Indolence is the greatest danger: your Companion is capable of arousing you from a lassitude of spirit and, to that end, if necessary, robbing you of your certainties, trampling on your secret gardens and, finally, tearing away the great veil of illusion.

It sometimes happens that your Companion is of the same sign as your year of birth, a twin brother in a way — for example, a Monkey/Monkey. In this case, you must recognize that he will compel you to realize yourself fully and to live the double aspect — the Yin and the Yang — that your bear within yourself. In any case, you also bear within yourself the twelve animals. So, set out on the long route, ready for the great adventure: the beautiful voyage during which you will encounter the harmoniously entangled, the solemn and the grotesque, the ephemeral reality, the dream and the imagined.

Table of hours corresponding to the twelve emblematic animals

If you were **born** between	11 pm and 1 am	your **companion** is	Rat
	1 am and 3 am		Ox
	3 am and 5 am		Tiger
	5 am and 7 am		Rabbit
	7 am and 9 am		Dragon
	9 am and 11 am		Snake
	11 am and 1 pm		Horse
	1 pm and 3 pm		Goat
	3 pm and 5 pm		Monkey
	5 pm and 7 pm		Rooster
	7 pm and 9 pm		Dog
	9 pm and 11 pm		Pig

These figures correspond to the *solar hour* of your birth. If necessary, you should check the summer times (Daylight Savings Time) and make the appropriate adjustment (sometimes two hours before or after statutory time).

THE MONKEY AND ITS COMPANION IN LIFE

 Monkey/Rat

Before leaving on a trip, these two should prepare a first-aid kit: their journey is more likely to resemble a hazardous adventure than an agreeable outing. These two Companions believe in the principle of 'an eye for an eye and a tooth for a tooth', and will repay each other accordingly. The Monkey will have but one idea — to devour the unhappy little rodent. The Rat will use all his tricks, including the most perverse, to cause his Companion to fall into physical, moral and even spiritual traps. These two strange companions will have no tenderness for each other and will give each other no respite. Their journey will be staged in a prize-fighting ring, where all blows are allowed and no rules are observed. May the stronger win!

 Monkey/Ox

You will not resist the Ox's charm nor his persuasive and sympathetic magic for very long. Some sound advice: if you want peace, create the illusion that he is the stronger, but be attentive and sympathetic as well. This courageous animal is remarkably agile; physically and mentally he is a first-rate acrobat, gifted with a rare power of persuasion. Take care: the Monkey is sometimes a sorcerer capable of transforming the power of the Ox into mere confetti and mirages.

Monkey/Tiger

Games of hide-and-seek, conjuring tricks and hoaxes will blend with feline stratagems and intrepidity. That sorcerer the Monkey has more than one trick up his sleeve — depend on him to transform you into a fearless tightrope walker or a dazzling juggler. As playful as the Goat, for him the game is a matter of getting you to accomplish what *he* has decided you should accomplish. The Monkey/Tiger is a formidable animal that, by combining the proud bearing and temperate skills of the Tiger with the ever-present wizardry of the little Monkey, can turn anything upside down and provoke many a sleepless night. For the Monkey, leaping unobserved from branch to branch in the jungle with his eyes shut, one cannot apply the usual formula, 'put a Tiger in your tank'. It will have to be, 'wrap a Tiger in the skin of a mischievous Monkey and then you will really see something!'

Monkey/Rabbit

He will be an inventive, lively, rather airy animal. He will have a tendency to be calculating, and will leave nothing to chance. He prefers being a schemer, conjuror and scrounger to labourious and irksome work. The Monkey/Rabbit envisages life as a game which, for the fun of it, he himself strews with traps and mirages, the better to zigzag between them. To attain his ends, he throws scruples to the wind. He will not hesitate to cheat, but who is he deceiving? He does not know himself, unless one day the Sphinx asks him the question.

THE MONKEY

Monkey/Dragon

Possessing a combination of the supremely gifted synchronized with a talent and taste for walking the tightrope, the Monkey/Dragon — a valiant and fearless guardian — will never unbuckle his armour. Always prepared for war, his days and nights are spent in a state of alertness, much to the continued astonishment of his friends. Alas, he tends to be an extortioner. He has charm, is brilliant and his intelligence is remarkable, but his main defect is his immoderate pride. His company is appreciated, but only in small doses. He will be a phenomenon and his collaboration and assistance will be desired, but you will not be able to breathe freely until you have seen the back of him. So, unwind a little, be natural and glance on your fellow creatures with a less condescending eye.

Monkey/Snake

He will be rational and a good organizer, but he will not be able to conceal his strong superiority complex which, unless he takes care, will cause him major problems. An intelligent and quick animal, his tendency to get carried away will be tempered by deep reflection; even so, he will always refuse to listen to the advice of others, because of his pride and self-esteem. He will not entertain any argument about his ideas, still less that his work or his word be questioned. The Monkey/Snake is talkative, courageous and, at times, a liar. However, his ability and his subtlety are major trump cards.

Monkey/Horse

In turn eloquent and courageous, his path will resemble an extended race-course, from which the Monkey/Horse can only emerge victorious. He will be as well-balanced as a race horse, at once mount and rider; a Don Juan or a hermit, — as well as having a touch of Don Quixote — transforming a track into an arena. He will stake his life — from pride, from a delight in taking risks and even from cynicism. Uniting intelligence with a fine appearance, he exploits to the utmost his resources of charm, talent, wiliness and, sometimes, deceit. The Monkey/Horse will often dream of a path haloed by glory and strewn with flowers — that he will stamp upon with superb indifference.

 Monkey/Goat

Intuitive and intelligent, he will be extremely restless. At times pride will curb his fantasies and his ideas will then gain in constancy and consistency, though there is no certainty that he really wants to prusue them to their logical end. The Monkey likes to leap from branch to branch, and the Goat leaps ceaselessly from cloud to cloud. Thus, their alliance will be particularly lively and eventful. As for love, the Monkey/Goat can be a real heartbreaker!

THE MONKEY

Monkey/Monkey

He will be by nature chivalrous, slightly boastful and often proud. He will have some difficulties in staying on a straight course; in fact, he will be tempted to take detours and shortcuts for the sheer pleasure of discovery and a taste for novelty. He cannot stay in one place and epitomizes the born traveller. If he comes across an obstacle, he will be tempted to get round it by using guile rather than by overcoming it directly. The Monkey/Monkey will be diabolically intelligent and lucid. However, though luck and happiness are apt to favour him, he will often be incapable of enjoying these gifts; he is too preoccupied with himself and blinded by a narcissism which will rob him of his best opportunities.

Monkey/Rooster

Very proud and full of himself, he will not be, to say the least, modest and self-effacing. He will see to it that he never goes unnoticed and will care a great deal about the effect he produces on others. Lacking neither intelligence nor good taste, he will still be irresistibly attracted by all that glitters. A word of advice: do not call too much attention to his weaknesses because the Monkey/Rooster will never forgive you!

Monkey/Dog

A supremely intuitive animal, it will be difficult to put him off his trail; he will always find his way despite obstacles and difficulties. However, he has a tendency to complicate his life because, to him, everything is a voyage. He hates simplicity, straight lines and mapped-out routes. The Monkey/Dog will often be a character with marked phases of exaltation and depression. Today full of spirit and sure of himself — even a little too much so — tomorrow he will see everything as completely black, questioning his projects, ideas and decisions. Avoid following him if you like to travel in peace.

Monkey/Pig

He will adept at living in solitude, an extremely clear-sighted person to whom it is inadvisable to talk humbug. In fact, he has a built-in lie-detector that sometimes resembles clairvoyance. He has a horror of speaking without purpose. The Monkey/Pig will not be easy to live with: he has his own conceptions of life and will not tolerate having others' imposed on him. He likes to bury his treasures — material or psychological — which are not always of a very clear origin. The Monkey/Pig has, at times, a rather peculiar idea of honesty.

THE MONKEY
AND THE FIVE
ELEMENTS

YOUR ELEMENT

In Chinese astrology, each year is joined to an Element. There are five Elements: *Water, Fire, Wood, Metal, Earth.*

Each of the twelve emblematic animals is linked successively to each of the five Elements. For example, in the year 1900 the Rat was Earth, in 1912 he was Fire; in 1924 he was Metal, in 1936, Water and in 1948 he was Wood. Therefore, for the twelve years from 1900 he was linked to Earth, for the next twelve years to Fire, and, for every succeeding period of twelve years, to each of the other Elements, in succession.

In order to determine the Element corresponding to the year of your birth, use the table below:

> *Years whose digits end in:* 1 and 6 — Water
>
> 2 and 7 — Fire
>
> 3 and 8 — Wood
>
> 4 and 9 — Metal
>
> 5 and 0 — Earth

The same union of *Animal-Element* repeats every sixty years, for example, Rat-Earth appeared in 1720, 1780, 1840, 1900, 1960 and so on.

The five Elements are the primary forces affecting the universe. It is their particular association with each of the signs which provides the basis for every horoscope. Movement and fluctuation, Yin and Yang, these symbolic forces are in a perpetual state of action and interaction.

Wood gives birth to Fire, which gives birth to Earth, which gives birth to Metal, which gives birth to Water, which in turn gives birth to Wood.

MONKEY/WATER
(you were born in 1956)

The cold born of the northern sky descended to earth and gave birth to Water. The Chinese consider Water more a synonym for coldness and ice than the source of heat and fertility.

Characteristics of the Monkey/Water

Water of winter nights, rigour and severity; calm and deep water to be feared and respected; still water sheltering demons asleep in its depths; fetid and muddy water of the marsh, the refuge of crawling creatures.

The Water Element will tend to confirm the Monkey's irrational impulses, thus cutting him off from the realities of the world and its constraints. The Monkey/Water perceives the world in a global and uncertain manner, through foggy and slightly confused vision. But the Monkey is both Yin and Yang, and it is in his power to enliven Water, to render it bracing and dynamic. Thus by his own power of will he can act upon this Element, inclining it towards the positive and the creative. So, Monkey/Water, find your source, then flee the marsh.

Health of the Monkey/Water

The Water organ is the kidney. Its flavour is salted. The Monkey is active and should remain so. If quiet waters attract him, he should be careful not to sail on them too often: they could be dangerous for his nervous and mental equilibrium.

The Monkey/Water and others

The Monkey/Water will be tolerant and thoughtful, capable of subduing his pride and of listening to others. He is inclined to moderation rather than excess, and will make his mark in a responsible position which he will assume calmly and serenely. However, this can be simply a game, another form of experience for the Monkey. He needs to test his potential and then the reactions of his friends. Yet he will almost never lose his sense of humour and detachment and will rarely take himself seriously. But boredom can sour his good humour and flights of fancy. The Monkey needs to communicate with men, to compel them to vibrate; he must lead them, if sometimes from a distance. The Monkey/Water will be more of a humanist than a mystic. His deepest anxiety is the boredom of routine and its stagnation.

Advice for a Monkey/Water

You need action, movement, change, novelty and discoveries. Respect your need to question everything because it is one of the keys to your success.

A Monkey/Water year

The culminating point for any Monkey/Water year will be winter, a period of gestation.

It is a year of ripening. Try not to preempt the harbingers of success, which bring in their wake the harvest and the fruits of your work. On the other hand, do not build on still waters: a groundwell may lurk beneath. In short, beware of the unforeseen: it can devastate you.

Historical example of a Monkey/Water year 1956

It does nobody any good to be Crown Prince for too long. This was undoubtedly true of Sir Anthony Eden: when he finally assumed his inheritance and became Prime Minister he had lost the nerve essential for the exercise of power.

When President Nasser of Egypt nationalized the Suez Canal on 26 July Eden regarded it as an affront, which it was intended to be, and as a direct and dangerous attack on the vital interests of Great Britain, which it was not.

For a period rarely before equalled the French and British governments conspired and connived together. The two former great powers were reliving, in unnatural harmony, their preoccupations of a century before. Protracted and diffuse negotiations ensued, based rather on legalistic rights and their moral and commercial appeal to other nations than on the priorities of national interest to which the two powers pretended, and the loss of which they greatly feared. A laborious military build-up accompanied these public discussions, Cyprus being the appointed launching place.

Nasser's policy presented an immediate and practical threat to the State of Israel, whose government accordingly joined secretly in the Anglo-French talks. Together they resolved on war. Initially the Israelis were to attack, affording the two Western powers a moral justification for 'putting out the forest fire', a phrase greeted with the derision it deserved when uttered by Eden on British television. The American reaction was prompt: a financial threat which Harold Macmillan, then Chancellor of the Exchequer, could not ignore. The power of the dollar was too great.

The hypocrisy of the Americans could be sustained; that of France and England could not. The Soviet Union, then engaged in ruthless suppression of a patriotic rising in Hungary, threatened more physical action. Eden gave in, followed quickly by the French. A truce was declared and the Allied Forces were withdrawn; the Israeli forces remained in the positions they had conquered.

MONKEY/WOOD
(you were born in 1908 or 1968)

To the East the wind blew in the sky, and from its warm caress of the earth Wood was born.

Characteristics of the Monkey/Wood

Wood is of the morning, springtime, temperate nature, loving harmony, beauty and elegance. This season will be fruitful and creative for the Monkey, bringing him equilibrium and creative power.

The Monkey/Wood will appreciate the art of living, be sensitive to nuances and tradition, and quite often will be an artist. Understanding and tolerant, he will be a humanist. When angry or impassioned, the Monkey/Wood will find quietness in nature and solitude to appease his anger and obsessions. The Wood Element will moderate the Monkey's abundant activity and offer him stability. His only fault: susceptibility.

Health of the Monkey/Wood
The organ of Wood is the liver; its flavour is acid. The Monkey/Wood sometimes needs to overcome his black moods and stop fussing about details. When he is really true to himself, the Monkey/Wood cannot only exercise a remarkable control over his deepest impulses, but also over his metabolism, for he knows how to listen to his body's needs. This will enable him to develop his will when very young.

The Monkey/Wood and others
The Monkey/Wood will often have an apparently relaxed attitude, but this will only be a facade, a technique for hiding his weaknesses and secret qualms. He will usually succeed, and few will guess at the conflicts and tensions at work behind his jovial and debonair mask. Against the rigidity of certain institutions, the Monkey/Wood will set his imagination and sense for improvization, and here he will work miracles. You will be convinced that he is perfectly sure of himself, relaxed, playing with words and circumstances. You will never suspect that he is in fact using a defensive technique so carefully constructed that it becomes in truth an art of living exemplified by an attention to detail and an insistence on perfection.

Advice for a Monkey/Wood
You know perfectly well how to cope with real difficulties, so do not question your abilities simply because the occasional wave rises around you.

A Monkey/Wood year

The culminating point in a Monkey/Wood year will be spring, the time of growth and prosperity.

A harmonious year in which you will be able to give free rein to your imagination and to your gift for life. However, control your weaknesses: do not allow your garden to be invaded, lest it become overrun with weeds.

Historical example of a Monkey/Wood year 1968

In 1968 the British and French governments were beset by a common problem, student unrest. Not for the first time, the students of Europe found their inspiration in the United States. The hybrids from the campuses flowered in England and in France; in both countries students attacked the authority of their teachers and of the university they were paid to attend. They campaigned against the politics of the politicians responsible for paying both the universities and their teachers to exercise authority over them and to teach them the rudiments of learning, trimmed by some old-fashioned refinements. The students, good anarchists at heart, considered the refinements out of date and thoroughly resented the rudiments.

The English government wisely refused to intervene directly. However, lest it should be accused of being wholly insensitive to the clamours of the young, it determined that they should be enfranchised at the age of 18, the silent argument being that those impelled by the offer of a grant to study should have the right to vote for those able to offer the grant. This enfranchisement was duly proclaimed by Act of Parliament.

In France it was a different story. De Gaulle, for whom barricades erected by students (or by anyone else) were little more than an historical coda to Parisian behaviour, was aloof to the pragmatic considerations which determined the actions of the Anglo-Saxons. Nor was he inclined to accept the advice of his Minister of Culture,

André Malraux, that a violent insurrection of students, in which the trade unions and the parties of the Left had joined, amounted to a veritable 'crisis of civilization', a calling into question of the traditional values of France. A noble and austere man, he vacillated, possibly for the first time in his life. He disappeared, but he did so to think. On 30 May he returned to Paris and then announced a referendum inviting the nation's support. He was given it. Later he was to say: 'I recovered myself and I recovered France.'

MONKEY/FIRE
(you were born in 1932)

Heat was born in the southern sky, descended to earth and fertilized it. From their union, Fire was born.

Characteristics of the Monkey/Fire

The Fire Element is of midday, of the South, of summer. Fire is Yang; it is the Element that heats, burns, transforms, confuses.

Fire will multiply the Monkey's energies, accentuating his need for perpetual movement; but Fire will also tend to consume much of his power. This is why the Monkey should avoid wasting his reserves of energy and squandering his resources, lest he destroy himself. He must learn to restrain himself and to control his overactive nature. This Fire could also be an inner fire, a devouring flame, keeping him on the alert but allowing him little time for sleep and recuperation. Luckily, the Monkey possesses the Yin tendency, a calming and balancing factor.

Health of the Monkey/Fire

The organ of Fire is the heart, its flavour is bitter. Avoid becoming entrapped by aggressiveness and anger to the point of all control; for then you will lose cohesion, dissipate your energies and be condemned to wander endlessly like a mad comet.

The Monkey/Fire and others

Fire is often synonymous with war. It is lucid and clairvoyant, but also violent, irascible and impassioned. You will certainly not be very diplomatic, and your aggressiveness will often win out. You are a man of action and leadership; you also cultivate a kind of tolerance and a vehement anti-conformism. Your fervour and your inner demands may press you towards the monkish solitude of a philosopher. The Monkey/Fire will seesaw between the satisfaction of his strong material needs and his mystical aspirations, tending at times to fanaticism, isolating him from his fellowmen and cutting him off from reality.

Advice for the Monkey/Fire

Businessman or mystic, allow your energies free rein but moderate your judgements and your actions with understanding and indulgence. Learn the meaning of the word 'tolerance'.

A Monkey/Fire year

The culminating point for a Monkey/Fire year will be summer, a period of creation. Your Yang tendency will be reinforced by the Yang of your Element, giving an abundance of energy.

A year full of action, surprises and forging ahead — the kind of year you like. However, do not lose your cohesion or you will spoil your chances, which are based on your strong will and good physical condition.

Historical example of a Monkey/Fire year 1812

By 1812 the French Empire had reached its greatest extent; its 152 departments contained fifty million of the one hundred and seventy five million of inhabitants of Europe. Yet this was the year which relieved England, Paymaster of Europe, in its attenuated struggle against Napoleon.

The accord with Russia, symbolized by the floating raft at Tilsit, had been abrogated. In 1810 the Tsar Alexander I found it necessary to discontinue his participation in the 'Continental System' by which Napoleon sought and very nearly managed to reduce Great Britain to starvation and surrender. The Russians, urgently needing industrial goods that the French were unable to provide, concluded an agreement covering preferential tariffs with the British. Napoleon was determined to assert the System of Tilsit and did so, at first by provocative action in Poland and Turkey, finally by military action against Russia itself. Securing levees from Prussia and Austria by demand rather than by negotiation, he assembled an army numerically larger than any previously recorded. But it lacked any natural cohesion. Its unwilling drafts, conscripted throughout Europe, were awed but not moved by Napoleon's aspirations. The Polish contingents possibly relished the prospect of revenge against a hereditary enemy; certainly, the armies of Austria flinched from the association. Imbued with the professional standards common in the eighteenth century, they had no sympathy for the system of total war conducted by Napoleon. They considered it barbaric and themselves to be dishonoured by participating in it.

However, Napoleon's object was not total war — he wanted a quick victory and a rapid peace. He misunderstood the Russians as he had misunderstood the Spanish. Dumbfounded and obstinate, he stayed on too long. He had counted on the niceties of diplomacy but by forgoing the formality of actually declaring war he forfeited every consideration.

MONKEY/EARTH
(you were born in 1920 or 1980)

Earth was born from the slowly falling Element of the sky at its humid zenith.

Characteristics of the Monkey/Earth
This is an afternoon Earth, the humid and hot Earth of summer. Earth is the symbol of a downy nest, of comfort and

abundance; of slow and profound transformations.

Like the eleven other emblematic animals, the Monkey is only passing through on Earth, but the Monkey/Earth will arrange things so that his stay will be as comfortable as possible; to this end no sacrifice will be too great. He will often be egotistical and proud, slightly forgetful of the Earth which carries him and which is a cauldron, the symbol of docility. In the best of cases, the Monkey/Earth will take refuge in his Element with the object of recharging his energies. But most of the time the Earth will be a lair — a cavern in which to bury his treasures rather than a temple for meditation.

The Monkey/Earth will be first and foremost a materialist, placing his imagination at the service of his need for power.

Health of the Monkey/Earth

The Earth's organ is the spleen, its flavour is sweet. The Monkey/Earth will remain active and keep a close eye on his weight. In fact, strongly inclined towards greediness and overeating, he will have a tendency to gain weight, above all in old age.

The Monkey/Earth and others

The Monkey/Earth is more pragmatic and realistic than the other Monkeys. All of his enterprises are motivated by an overriding need for expansion and a desire for an increasing number of possessions. But he also likes activities that bear fruit and will be attracted to speculation, banking and real estate — in short, tangible values. His main preoccupation will be the accumulation of goods, the harvesting and gathering of crops. The Monkey/Earth will often be distrustful and suspicious of those near to him, which will sometimes make him difficult to live with. He is easily worried about his future, and will be constantly tormented by his need to be financially secure. He cannot, however, be reproached for his lack of courage: his fortune is always built by the sweat of his brow and at the price of laborious and conscientious work. With the Monkey/Earth, greed has its roots in fear, and is all the more intense because this fear of insecurity is buried deeply in his unconscious.

Advice for the Monkey/Earth

Dreams have no value on the stock market and weigh little in the balance; but they are the honey that is the balm for our wounds. So, keep a secret garden in which to cultivate your dreams; they will soothe your anxiety more than all the gold in Fort Knox.

A Monkey/Earth year

The culminating point for a Monkey/Earth will be summer, the season of hot and humid soil. Your savings account and barns will be full, so turn your eyes towards the summits or the starry canopy of heaven. Profit from this period to widen your perspective and discover new horizons.

Historical example of a Monkey/Earth year 1260

The idea of universality in human affairs still held good in the late thirteenth century. The Papacy was still infused with the concept of a Christian dominion; the Angevins sought to dominate the Mediterranean world and aspired to the conquest of the Byzantine Empire; the Mongol Empire attained its apogee with the reign of Koubilai, who assumed the throne in 1260, thirty-three years after the death of Ghenghis Khan. Tibet had been absorbed and the armies of Batou had penetrated Finland. Hougalou, the brother of Koubilai, captured and sacked Baghdad and asserted his dominion.

Yet Koubilai brought order and prosperity, even an apparent stability, to his immense empire. He was a great administrator and capable of valuable innovations. He understood about cities, a priceless asset for his subjects in the West; and not only did he organize their development, he also arranged for their citizens the human necessities of urban life. He introduced paper money, a remarkable experiment for his day, built hospitals, and funded care for the sick and the poor. He opened schools and established a national alphabet. On a scale almost equal to the Romans he constructed roads and canals throughout his empire. He also paid his armies on a regular basis, thus securing their obedience while restraining their greed. Since his administration was orderly it was accepted as just, and his levies were carefully related to the income of his subjects rather than to their capital wealth.

Marco Polo, reporting on these aspects of Koubilai's empire to the Venetians, is said to have been met by a total incredulity: the sophisticated Venetians could not understand how 'barbarian hordes' could so rapidly absorb the elements of an ancient civilization. Yet the Normans had already done so a century before in their Kingdom of Sicily.

MONKEY/METAL
(you were born in 1944)

In the sky, coming from the West, drought grazed the skin of the earth and gave birth to Metal. Winds come from the faraway steppes, seeking the vital sap.

Characteristics of the Monkey/Metal

Metal is of the night, of the autumn and of cold. It symbolizes clarity, purity and firmness. Metal is decisive; it cuts through; its temperament is rigid and chaste; its remarks stinging. It oscillates between beauty and destruction. In other respects, it is expert at putting plans into effect. At harvest time it is the blade that gleans. Alas, too much rigour engenders sadness and moroseness.

The Monkey/Metal will often be unsatisfied. He will be apt to look for the impossible, the inaccessible, and will often be attracted to mysticism and have a tendency to shut himself off. Removing himself from the world and from life, he will suffer from his inability to deal with the day-to-day struggle. Paradoxically, the Monkey/Metal loves glittering success; he feels the desire to lead, supervise and control, and in these he is formidable. He is uncompromising, inflexible, sometimes even fanatical. The Metal Element will often be dangerous for the Monkey by enclosing him in a rigid armour and restraining him; sometimes imposing upon him a way of life, rules of conduct and ethics so that the Monkey will lose his freedom of movement, if not his liberty. This is a kind of straitjacket in which he may suffer and be destroyed.

Health of the Monkey/Metal

Metal's organ is the lungs, their flavour is pungent. Since summits of all kinds attract you, take to mountain climbing. But above all, control your breathing; it is the key to your equilibrium.

The Monkey/Metal and others

The Monkey/Metal will aim for high positions and great responsibilities, but he will need diversity and innovation in his work. He will not tolerate the routine of the daily grind. He will be an inventor, but the Monkey's imagination will often be subordinate to rigour and severity. Mixing the exigent with the meticulous, he will have a tendency to make abrupt decisions. Rather stiffnecked and obstinate for a Monkey, he will not accept compromises easily.

The Monkey/Metal may be a remarkable man of law, whether a judge or practising lawyer — but he will be neither obliging nor flexible. He will apply the law, statute or article strictly. He often behaves in an enigmatic and closed manner: besides his repugnance for explaining and justifying himself, he is prompted by a constant desire to stand apart and to be different, from which comes a taste for solitude and some difficulty in communicating with his fellows.

Advice for the Monkey/Metal

You suffer from your isolation and your narrow-mindedness, so make an effort to come down to earth; soften your judgements and burst open the iron collar of your prejudices. Rules that are too austere generate anguish and disorder.

A Monkey/Metal year

The culminating point for a Monkey/Metal year will be autumn. The Yin tendency of the midseason will balance the Yang of the Monkey, encouraging tolerance and moderation.

This year will be the symbol of openness and flexibility, so lay down your arms, soften your movements and round off the corners; freedom of gesture and of heart will bring you a breath of fresh air.

Do not prevent yourself from breathing freely because you wish to demonstrate your self-control; you will only reveal your narrow-mindedness when great liberation is within your reach.

Historical example of a Monkey/Metal year 1944

This was the climactic year of the Second World War and should have seen the end of it in the west. According to plan, and by coincidence on the same day, 6 June, the Russian summer offensive coincided with the Allied invasion of Europe. By 25 July the Russian armies had destroyed 25 divisions of the German armies and were advancing to the Vistula. On 19 August General de Gaulle entered Paris to a triumphant reception disturbed but, in its enthusiasm, not diminished by intermittent sniping from the rooftops. For this he owed much to the chivalry and good sense of the German commander who refused to act on orders from Berlin to desecrate the city; also, to his courage, for it was a brave man who refused to carry out orders after the failure of the Stauffenburg plot to kill Hitler on 19 July.

More serious sniping followed between the Allied generals and their governments. Field Marshal Montgomery, in the tradition of Marlborough, appreciated that the essential problem lay in supply, particularly in the supply of petrol for the armoured groups. He pressed for a single deep thrust into the Ruhr, Germany's industrial heart. He would necessarily have been in command of the operation and in command of American armies for the purpose. The idea was politically unacceptable to the Americans and the suggestion resented by their generals whose troops out-numbered the British. The supreme commander, General Eisenhower, had no choice. He could neither accept the British plan nor release his own forces for a single thrust to the south of the Ruhr. Moreover, Montgomery's ability to strike fast was suspect and Patton, the best tank general on either side after Rommel's death, would not have served under him. A general advance was therefore ordered. Predictably, the supplies available were insufficient to support it.

Retribution followed. Ignoring the lessons of history the Ardennes was left lightly defended by the Allied command. In effect, their armies had gone into winter quarters. On 12 December the German panzers broke through and threatened to re-enact the great manoeuvre of 1940.

As so often happens, the threat of disaster bought cohesion to the Allies. Montgomery assumed command of all forces in the area and deployed them with precision. The Americans held out courageously and bought time at Bastogne; and Patton himself executed a rapid redeployment of which any other general would have been incapable of contemplating. Even so the Allies were lucky. The panzers missed the great petrol dump which alone could have taken them to the Channel. The attack petered out. The alarm was over.

Alarm it was, but the outcome of the battle would not have affected the outcome of the war. More significant for the future was President Roosevelt's withdrawal from the Morgenthau plan which would have reduced Germany to an agrarian economy after victory had been won.

Analogical Table
of the Different Elements

Elements	Wood	Fire	Earth	Metal	Water
Years ending in	3 and 8	2 and 7	0 and 5	4 and 9	1 and 6
Colours	Green	Red	Yellow	White	Blue
Seasons	Spring	Summer	End of summer	Autumn	Winter
Climates	Wind	Heat	Humid	Dry	Cold
Flavours	Acid	Bitter	Sweet	Pungent	Salty
Principal organ	Liver	Heart	Spleen	Lungs	Kidneys
Secondary organ	Gallbladder	Small intestine	Stomach	Large intestine	Bladder
Food	Wheat, poultry	Rice, lamb	Corn, beef	Oats, horse	Peas, pork

Table of Harmony Between the Elements

	Wood Female	Fire Female	Earth Female	Metal Female	Water Female
Male Wood	●●	○	○○○	○	○○
Male Fire	○	○	○○	●	●●
Male Earth	●●	○○	○○○	○○○	●
Male Metal	○	●●	●	●●	○○○
Male Water	○○	●●	●	○○○	○

○○○ Excellent prosperity

○○ Good harmony, understanding

○ Effort needed

● Rivalries and problems of reciprocal domination

●● Misunderstanding and incomprehension

THE
FOUR SEASONS
OF
THE MONKEY

If you were born in spring
Monkey/Aries

It is good for a Monkey to be born under the sign of Aries, just as it is good for an Aries to be born in a Monkey year. However, those born under the sign of Aries are sometimes too frank and too instinctive. They have a tendency to rush into things whatever the visibility, without taking heed of the weather forecast. The Monkey is crafty and intelligent; he never loses sight of his best interests. His opportunism will lend increased efficiency to the active Aries and the latter will endow the Monkey with a basic honesty, for which his friends can only be thankful.

The Monkey/Aries is capable of making total use of the many resources of these two emblematic animals. A born fighter — at times skilful and diplomatic, at others taking dangerous risks in order to impress his public — he is extremely resourceful in business, capable of keeping several irons in the fire at the same time and carrying on several conversations simultaneously. He has a good memory and will not make the same mistake more than once. He is brilliant, direct and seductive. He is courageous and has a flair for recognizing and assessing danger; he is a strategist as well as a fighter.

Monkey/Taurus

This Monkey is a far cry from a marmoset; he is, rather, a member of the gorilla or orangoutang species. For a Monkey he is slow and reflective. He is also sentimental and capable of covering up his escapades with the help of some pious lies; when he lies, it is with the best intentions in the world. The Monkey and Taurus both have a good business sense, and their alliance will strengthen it considerably. It also strengthens his memory, while diminishing a tendency towards fantasy and the dispersion of energies.

The Monkey/Taurus is sociable and enjoys life. He is a born possessor: as soon as he sees something which pleases him, he wants to have it. If he does not get what he wants through his work, he will exploit his cleverness, ready to bend the rules a little. In any case, he will lack for nothing. He is as gifted at earning money as he is at spending it; he will not let his gold lie in a bank vault. He could be a broker or a brilliant speculator. Endowed with a practical and constructive intelligence, he has the capacity to deepen his knowledge and put it to good use. On the emotional level, he will do well to marry an heiress.

Monkey/Gemini

We have seen how delicate a task it is to find analogies between the Western and the Chinese zodiacs. With perhaps one other exception, the Monkey and Gemini are so alike that one could be mistaken for the other. This alliance therefore represents the 'pure Monkey' or the 'pure Gemini'. All of his qualities and defects are magnified: he is remarkably intelligent (if you meet an illiterate Monkey/Gemini, take him immediately to have an IQ test — you may be rendering society a great service), high-spirited, eclectic, quick-witted, resourceful and eloquent. He is also nervous, unstable, flighty, lacks perseverance and concentration and is often flying off in several directions at once.

If you fall in love with a male or female Monkey/Gemini, try to tolerate their escapades: their passions never last. And you will be repaid in a few years because the Monkey/Gemini becomes the most charming, liveliest and youthful of old people.

If you were born in summer
Monkey/Cancer

The Monkey's activity is, as a general rule, essentially mental; that of Cancer, emotional. The former experiences only surface emotions; the second feels deeply. The individual who has within himself these contradictory tendencies — if he is not a genius, and that is a rare breed — may feel himself to be like an animal derived from two different species.

It is important to the Monkey/Cancer that he control his life rather than submit to it. In the latter case, he will become a wanderer, unstable and suffering from his instability, always frustrated emotionally and a bit of an obsessive liar. In the former case, on the other hand, the Monkey/Cancer, if he adapts himself to the possibility of making use of the qualities of the two signs, will not allow himself to be overcome by hypersensitivity and will retain the perspective necessary to have a healthy view of life. He will then succeed in his professional life without making too many enemies (thanks to the soothing influence of Cancer), and be capable of a successful love-life, and even fidelity, something difficult for all Monkeys.

Monkey/Leo

Except for his appearance, he is a savage baboon. To understand this, look at the monkeys in a zoo. You will see that they are formidable, having long, sharp teeth over which they draw back the lips of a wild animal. They do not hesitate to attack and appear to take themselves with the utmost seriousness. The Monkey/Leo is the same. It is inadvisable to pull his mane, and before starting a discussion with him it is best to prepare one's arguments carefully and to refresh one's knowledge of the Classics. Address him formally and assume a respectful air when approaching him; and, naturally, avoid contradicting him, as he will not take this lightly. The Monkey/Leo seems physically large, even if he is actually quite short and slim. You can be sure that he has the means to get what he wants; he is cultivated, brilliant and exceedingly well-informed. His vital energy equals his vivacity of mind: he is both head and feet.

Monkey/Virgo

Here, nervousness is the dominating factor. Deep inside himself the Monkey/Virgo is in turmoil, but he forces himself to present an outwardly stable appearance and to keep solid control of himself. This constant battle to maintain his equilibrium is as fatiguing as the twelve tasks of Hercules. He is not particularly malleable; in fact, he is as taut as a violin string. In him, perfectionism and fantasy, the strictest honesty and the wildest tricks confront each other constantly. He may have unsuspected reactions, sometimes prudish and moralizing, at others imaginative and provoking.

The positive side of this alliance is his kindness. The Monkey is sociable and has an engaging manner; he helps Virgo to overcome his timidity and to forget the small bag of complexes that he has dragged along with him since childhood. Virgo's feeling of inferiority and the Monkey's sense of superiority create an equilibrium in which Virgo's qualities of devotion can be seen to their greatest practical advantage. To sum up, the Monkey/Virgo, although often ill-at-ease, is perhaps the least dangerous to love, all the more because he has an excellent understanding of reality and is a capable and lucid worker.

If you were born in autumn
Monkey/Libra

A lengthy and thorough search among all of the combinations of the Eastern and Western astrologies will not reveal an alliance as sociable as the Monkey/Libra. He is an open, amiable, engaging and eloquent individual who is never more at ease than in the role of intermediary or of public relations consultant. In his hands the worst conflicts are always resolved. This he does, almost before you can look twice at him, with a few engaging words and a good deal of conciliation. One can well imagine him discoursing on world peace or walking about waving a banner inscribed, 'Come to me, I will arrange everything.' And it is true that he has a gift for arranging things. Behind a lighthearted and somewhat offhand exterior, he is humane, alert and available.

Of course he has his faults, but they are not big ones. This Monkey is very easy to live with. One piece of advice however: if you do not like background noise, buy ear plugs, for he never stops talking — about everything and nothing.

Monkey/Scorpio

As with the Monkey/Virgo, nervousness dominates, but here it is deeper. The Monkey/Scorpio is in a state of permanent anxiety and poses questions about everything and everybody. He surprises with his cynical attitude, his sombre side, which will suddenly explode into a thousand particles of fantasy. He is an intelligent being of foolproof lucidity who, when caught up in an activity or an emotion, always gives the impression that he is playing in a tragicomedy in which he is both actor and spectator.

The Monkey/Scorpio is gifted with an unlimited curiosity and a remarkable capacity for assimilation. Everything that is hidden, mysterious or complicated interests him. He would make a fine detective, an implacable and wily strategist, knowing in advance the tactics which could be turned to account: there should always be a Monkey/Scorpio in government to foresee and analyse the methods of the opposition. A piece of advice if you love him: buy a bulletproof vest; you will need it to survive his stings. It is not that he is disagreeable, but he cannot keep from criticizing and taking things apart just 'to see'.

Monkey/Sagittarius

This is an excellent alliance for a politician, a diplomat, or, better still, an ambassador. More modestly, careers such as those in a large-scale commercial undertaking are favourable. The Monkey/Sagittarius has good sense, lucidity tempered by a good nature, a perspicacity moderated by indulgence. Who can ask for more? Besides, he asks fewer questions than other Monkeys, being more intent on realizing his ambitions. Extremely sociable, but none too selective, he never feels so at home as when in the middle of a talkative and excited group. Interest the Monkey/Sagittarius in tourism, and in no time he will have trailing behind him a group of top businessmen out on a spree.

Very easy to live with for those who resemble him, he is frantically independent and has a strong predilection for action. On the other hand, if you are a sensitive, sentimental little thing, avoid him like the Plague: you will break your gold teeth on him. In fact, it is absolutely impossible to attach this Monkey to his perch. He needs wide-open windows in order to be happy.

If you were born in winter
Monkey/Capricorn
Those born under the sign of the Monkey are not simple people. If Capricorn is added, such a special cocktail is made that, even in noting down all the ingredients, it would be difficult to make it again. If it is Capricorn who dominates, his rigid influence risks freezing the Monkey into a sort of stereotyped fantasy. If the Monkey is the stronger there results a social — albeit tremendously selective — individual, excessively observant, uneasy, distrustful and nervous: in equal measure he is intelligent and, without repudiating his real nature, adaptable.

His behaviour can alternate between icy immobility and feverish activity. His attitude towards money is ambiguous: times he is sordidly avaricious, at others he throws money out of the window. In fact, he is hopeless about finding himself, knowing who he is or creating his own unity. He is, in general, more balanced in maturity than in adolescence: like wine, he grows better with age. He lacks neither courage nor ability, but his unconcerned, even unfeeling, appearance discourages some people.

Monkey/Aquarius
The Monkey/Aquarius is endowed with a remarkable ingenuity and an inventiveness without equal. He has something about him of the sorcerer's apprentice and of the hypnotizer; or the scholar or scientist who is unappreciated because he is ahead of his time. As a child, it is the Monkey/Aquarius who terrorizes his neighbourhood with barbarous

devices and regularly detonates 'bombs' in the cellar of the house. But do not dismiss him completely: under his roguish little face smeared with soot may lie the brain of an Einstein. With him, however, the end result is unpredictable: with his agile fingers he will create either a rocket or a wire to cut butter. Give him the benefit of the doubt.

Charming, pleasant, somewhat absentminded but always ready to listen to confidences, the Monkey/Aquarius is an agreeable companion, but not of much help if you are in need of security. Basically, he needs too much reassurance himself to be able to reassure others. He is an investigator, but to be effective he needs, as do all investigators, materials, recognition and three meals a day. He is an intellectual, not a businessman. Like the road to hell, his is paved with good intentions.

Monkey/Pisces

Elusive, floating here and there, slipping cunningly through the mesh of a net, here is the delicious Monkey/Pisces. He is utterly charming, persuasive and adaptable to an incredible degree; parachuted into high society, he will seem to be as at ease there as in a Ukrainian farm or a colony of penguins. He knows instinctively how to adopt the language suited to the occasion and the attitude required; he is a chameleon. Do not forget that the Monkey is an animal with a remarkable gift for imitation. The supple Pisces amplifies this tendency which comes close to mimicry. The Monkey/Pisces often loses his way. He is a specialist in unanswerable questions and metaphysical interrogations. It would not take much for him to forget to eat.

The Monkey/Pisces is a willing helper, but he is careful to guard his own little world. He hates to be confined, so, if you want to keep him, buy him a pretty cage — with the door left open — or, even better, an aquarium opening into the sea. He will reappear regularly, flapping his fins, and perhaps he will bring you the treasure from a sunken galleon — or an old shoe. He is so very unpredictable!

THE
I CHING

易经

THE I CHING AND THE MONKEY

In the I Ching game, you ask a question and you obtain an answer. It is therefore a divining game. But the question you ask is posed through your Monkey identity; the wheels, the complex mechanism of your mind and spirit, begin to turn. You ask a Monkey question and the I Ching answers with a Monkey 'solution', on which you then meditate as a Monkey before arriving at a Monkey conclusion.

The player is presented with a hexagram which contains the 'hypothesis-response' to his question, or, more exactly, a synthesis of forces affecting the concern or event inquired about.

For you, Master Monkey, here are the sixty-four hexagrams of the I Ching and sixty-four Monkey hypotheses.

How to proceed
1. The question
Ask a question regarding any problem at all, past, present or future, personally concerning you. (If the question concerns a friend, consult the I Ching game in the book corresponding to his Chinese sign.)

2. Method of play
It must be done with concentration.

Take **three ordinary and similar coins** — for example, three 50p coins.

Heads will equal the number 3.

Tails will equal the number 2.

Throw the coins.

If the result is two coins showing Heads and one Tails, write 3 + 3 + 2. You thus obtain a total of 8 which you represent by a continuous line: ———— .

Draw the same continuous line if you have three coins showing Heads (3 + 3 + 3 = 9).

If you throw two coins showing Tails and one Heads
(2 + 2 + 3 = 7), or all three showing Tails (2 + 2 + 2 = 6), draw
two separate lines: ▬ ▬ .

To sum up, 8 and 9 correspond to: ▬▬▬▬ (Yin)

6 and 7 correspond to: ▬ ▬ (Yang)

Repeat this operation *six times*, noting at the time of each
throw the figure obtained on a piece of paper, proceeding
from the first to the sixth figure, from bottom to top.

The final result, including a trigram from the bottom, or

lower trigram (example: ▬▬), and a trigram of the top,

or upper trigram (example: ▬▬), will be a hexagram of
the I Ching. In our example this would look like:

Now merely look for the hexagram number in the table on
page 82 , and then consult the list of hexagrams with their
descriptions to find the given answer. *In our example*, the
hexagram obtained is number 63, entitled **After completion**.

THE HEXAGRAMS OF THE MONKEY

CH'IEN

1 *The creative:* Energy, strength and will. Monkey of the irrational, often immune to reality, you will need much patience and tenacity to carry out your projects.

K'UN

2 *The receptive:* Do not neglect or scorn your tools; let them guide your hand; follow your intuition.

CHUN

3 *The initial difficulty:* Practise introspection. Listen to what lies deep within you; you will thus lift the veil of confusion.

MÊNG

4 *Youthful folly:* 'It is not I who seek the young fool but the young fool who seeks me.' You who hold masters in contempt, do not set yourself up as a master. In order to eliminate danger, it is not enough simply to deny it.

HSÜ

5 *Waiting:* Difficult for a Monkey who cannot stand still; you must, however, be resigned and know how to make the best of it.

SUNG

6 *Conflict:* Try to reach an amicable arrangement. This way of going about things agrees much more with your nature than do quarrels and confrontations.

Table of Hexagrams

Trigrams	Upper lines ☰	☷	☳
Lower lines			
☰	1	11	34
☷	12	2	16
☳	25	24	51
☵	6	7	40
☶	33	15	62
☴	44	46	32
☲	13	36	55
☱	10	19	54

Use this table to find the number of your hexagrams. The meeting point between the lower and upper trigrams indicates the number of the hexagram that you are seeking.

☵	☶	☴	☳	☱
5	26	9	14	43
8	23	20	35	45
3	27	42	21	17
29	4	59	64	47
39	52	53	56	31
48	18	57	50	28
63	22	37	30	49
60	41	61	38	58

SHIH

7 *The army:* A little discipline never harmed anyone. In any case, the Monkey is skilled in the art of getting round the rules and using them to his own advantage.

PI

8 *Holding together (union):* You will only win through unity. Your true power lies in your capacity for bringing people together.

SHIAO CH'U

9 *The taming power of the small:* Little streams make big rivers. Neglect no detail. The stream's murmur is sometimes enough to launch an avalanche.

LÜ

10 *Treading:* 'Tread on the tail of the Tiger, he does not bite man.' The king Monkey will not allow himself to be intimidated; however, pirouettes and tricks are indispensable to him.

T'AI

11 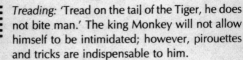 *Peace:* Accept the harmony of contraries. The Yin and Yang Monkey should understand the principle of alternation, but neither seek to explain it nor confine it within a cast-iron rational structure.

P'I

12 *Standstill:* Even if it is painful for you, it will be a wise counsellor. Before jumping onto a branch, make sure that it is not rotten.

T'UNG JÊN

13 *Fellowship with men:* The Monkey understands this very well, but not necessarily in broad daylight, as advised by the I Ching. Beware of schemes, deceptive intrigues and obscure sidestreets.

TAYU

14 *Possession in great measure:* Possession is only a means and not an end. The Monkey prefers to eat the fruit rather than to help it grow.

CH'IEN

15 *Modesty:* Symbol of moderation, equilibrium, stability. Difficult for the Monkey who is perpetually agitated. His agility should serve the equitable.

YÜ

16 *Enthusiasm:* You have the gift of gab, but the day always comes when the magician must explain his tricks — even if he loses some of his prestige and mystery.

SUI

17 *Following:* Thanks to your seductive charm, you have entered the queen's orchard. But do not misuse this charm: it will not extricate you from perilous or ambiguous situations forever.

KU

18 *Work on what has been spoiled:* If you sometimes vent a devious wit, at least do not indulge your pleasantries so far as to provoke a breach; you could be the first victim.

LIN

19 *Approach:* According to the principle of alternation, today's good fortune is likely to turn against you tomorrow.

KUAN

20 *Contemplation:* The Monkey likes to climb to the tops of trees or to the summit of a mountain less to appreciate the landscape than to be conspicuous and visible from afar. Take care: you are a marvellous target.

SHIH HO

21 *Biting through (or clearly defined penalties):* Become a little like a gorilla: sharpen your cutting teeth in preparation. The lie is familiar to you, but its consequences may be fatal.

PI

22 *Grace:* You possess many gift-wrapped presents; do not hesitate to offer them. Your gifts — abstract or material — will be repaid a hundred times over.

PO

23 *Splitting apart:* Despite a taste for risk, do not install yourself in a castle whose walls threaten to collapse.

FU

24 *Return — the turning point:* The prodigal Monkey. After the shadows comes light. Know how to turn back before going too far.

WU WANG

25 *Innocence:* It is not exactly your outstanding virtue, however, you will need it. Avoid devious schemes and complicated calculations.

TA CH'U

26 *The taming power of the great:* Power and success, on condition that you know how to renew your character. The Monkey will be in his element: everything should smile on him.

I

27 *The corners of the mouth:* Mentally, the Monkey is forever hungry. But, like the boa, his digestive capacity is prodigious — happily for him, since his appetite is limitless.

TA KUO

28 *Preponderance of the great:* To leap correctly from branch to branch, you must feel free in your movements. So, do not take on too much, even to amaze the audience.

K'AN

29 *The fathomless water:* It laps all around you. Be vigilant, and remember that the straightest route is always the shortest.

LI

30 *The clinging, fire:* Prestige, fortune and power are illusory golden prisons: it is better to avoid such enclosures than to be reduced to looking feverishly for the key.

HSIEN

31 *Influence:* You exercise a certain fascination, and in conversation easily cast a spell on those with you. Take advantage of this to win new adherents, renew commitments and strengthen alliances. Everything depends on your powers of persuasion.

HÊNG

32 *Duration:* You who are lucid should first of all be lucid about yourself; in this way you will avoid becoming too set in your ways and obtain better results. Even your charm will be more effective.

TUN

33 *Retreat:* Should be done quietly, without constraint or any feeling of impotence or guilt. It is a veritable art, sometimes a master stroke which represents an enormous victory.

TA CHUANG

34 *The power of the great:* Although you are extremely flexible and agile — the symbol of perpetual movement — it is in your interest to place a safety net beneath you before you jump; without it, the void may swallow you up.

CHIN

35 *Progress:* You are going to be able to make use of your gifts in broad daylight, but do not refuse to share the glory with your collaborators for fear they may eclipse you.

MING I

36 *Darkening of the light:* Being solely responsible, you must seek the cause within yourself. Light the candles or wait for dawn, but do not count on outside help; no one is going to bring you a light bulb.

CHIA JÊN

37 *The family:* The Monkey has a rather patriarchal view of the family: he has to assume all of the duties, and also all of the obligations.

K'UEI

38 *Opposition:* You often speak of tolerance and harmony; bring these words from your heart and remember that reconciliations are always possible.

CHIEN

39 *Obstruction:* Or the courage to face an ordeal. You can obtain some pleasure from this by proving that nothing can stop you; but do not overestimate your strength; do not tempt the devil.

HSIEH

40 *Deliverance:* After the thorns, here, at last, are the flowers! Take advantage of this to relax and wholeheartedly enjoy the harmony.

SUN

41 *Decrease:* The Monkey does not relish hard times. He will, however, know how to cheer himself up with superfluous and charming little nothings. Graceful and artistic poverty suits him better than boring and routine comfort. He will always enjoy a candlelit dinner, even though the plates are bare.

I

42 *Increase:* You are going to be forced to be opportunistic. How else can you blossom? You will not be told twice.

KUAI

43 *Breakthrough:* The curtain is about to rise; make your entrance. The Monkey will take malicious pleasure in exposing error or causing scandal; he never hesitates to pour oil on the fire.

KOU

44 *Coming to meet:* Do not associate with the flawed; distrust still waters — they reflect a false image and often flatter an image of which you are the first to be taken in.

TS'UI

45 *Gathering together:* Get rid of the hangers-on and concentrate your available energies. New and fruitful ideas will be born from them.

SHÊNG

46 *Pushing upwards:* Even if you climb to the top of the mountain faster than anyone else, take time to pause and catch your breath in the resting places provided. Before leaving, do not forget to check your equipment carefully.

K'UN

47 *Oppression:* You are losing liveliness and tone. Instead of prancing up and down, take the opportunity to recuperate. But take care: do not pretend to have recovered your confidence if you remain depressed.

CHING

48 *The well:* There are times in which to turn everything upside down and to question everything, and others to put everything in its place and restore order. Do not rely on others to take responsibility; you alone know your real needs.

KO

49 *Revolution:* It has its place in the indispensable cycle of alternation, and sometimes its logic proves inescapable; but do not make a dogma of it, for it will turn against you.

TING

50 *The cauldron:* Symbol of all five Elements — Earth, Wood, Fire, Water and Metal. Nourishment for the body and the mind. One must understand and respect the mysteries of this delicate alchemy.

CHÊN

51 *The arousing (shock, thunder):* The Monkey will know how to profit from ordeals; he has often emerged the victor, if at the price of executing some particularly acrobatic and painful pirouettes.

KÊN

52 *Keeping still:* Even though you need constant excitement and people around you, you will have to seek equilibrium in solitude and meditation. Accept reality; live for the present. Your inward commitment to things is the token of your success.

CHIEN

53 *Development (gradual progress):* As with the hare and the tortoise, it is enough to leave on time — and useless to tread on the head of your competitor.

KUEI MEI

54 *The bride:* 'Fortune and happiness', the Monkey will declare. 'On condition', Prudence will reply.

FÊNG

55 *Abundance:* To gorge oneself on all the fruit from the orchard, while preparing for an imminent journey across the desert.

LÜ

56 *The wanderer:* Very favourable to the Monkey, provided he abandons all ideas of conquest and gives serious thought to his destination. Take to the road; be free of ties and dependencies.

SUN

57 *The gentle:* Symbol of wind and clouds. The Monkey should feel at ease. He will insinuate himself, nip in and out everywhere; the least chink will suffice. He will end by surreptitiously triumphing over even the worst influences.

TUI

58 *The serene, the joyous:* It is the time for sharing and the joy it brings.

HUAN

59 *Dissolution:* Conquer egotism. This promises to be a rough battle requiring an exceptionally ardent spirit.

CHIEH

60 *Limitation:* This should be like a dressing on a wound. It is a technique, no more, but is better than gangrene, or amputation.

CHUNG FU

61 *Inner truth:* Your attitude alone should bear witness to it, so put away your suave words and cajoling airs.

HSIAO KUO

62 *Preponderance of the small:* Even though you dream of using extreme measures, you must content yourself with the options available to you at the moment. If shipwrecked — even if you have thrown a bottle into the sea — you should think seriously about how you are going to survive. Help does not fall from the sky.

CHI CHI

63 *After completion:* Maturity, plenitude, perfect equilibrium, but there is always a precipice nearby. If you leap, do not forget that you must yield to the laws of gravity.

WEI CHI

64 *Before completion:* Do not crown yourself nor proclaim yourself emperor, even if you sometimes take yourself for Napoleon.

General table of the years corresponding to the Chinese signs

THE RAT	THE OX	THE TIGER
31.1.1900/18.2.1901	19.2.1901/ 7.2.1902	8.2.1902/28.1.1903
18.2.1912/ 5.2.1913	6.2.1913/25.1.1914	26.1.1914/13.2.1915
5.2.1924/24.1.1925	25.1.1925/12.2.1926	13.2.1926/ 1.2.1927
24.1.1936/10.2.1937	11.2.1937/30.1.1938	31.1.1938/18.2.1939
10.2.1948/28.1.1949	29.1.1949/16.2.1950	17.2.1950/ 5.2.1951
28.1.1960/14.2.1961	15.2.1961/ 4.2.1962	5.2.1962/24.1.1963
15.2.1972/ 2.2.1973	3.2.1973/22.1.1974	23.1.1974/10.2.1975
2.2.1984/19.2.1985	20.2.1985/ 8.2.1986	9.2.1986/28.1.1987

THE RABBIT	THE DRAGON	THE SNAKE
29.1.1903/15.2.1904	16.2.1904/ 3.2.1905	4.2.1905/24.1.1906
14.2.1915/ 2.2.1916	3.2.1916/22.1.1917	23.1.1917/10.2.1918
2.2.1927/22.1.1928	23.1.1928/ 9.2.1929	10.2.1929/29.1.1930
19.2.1939/ 7.2.1940	8.2.1940/26.1.1941	27.1.1941/14.2.1942
6.2.1951/26.1.1952	27.1.1952/13.2.1953	14.2.1953/ 2.2.1954
25.1.1963/12.2.1964	13.2.1964/ 1.2.1965	2.2.1965/20.1.1966
11.2.1975/30.1.1976	31.1.1976/17.2.1977	18.2.1977/ 6.2.1978
29.1.1987/16.2.1988	17.2.1988/ 5.2.1989	6.2.1989/26.1.1990

THE HORSE	THE GOAT	THE MONKEY
25.1.1906/12.2.1907	13.2.1907/ 1.2.1908	2.2.1908/21.1.1909
11.2.1918/31.1.1919	1.2.1919/19.2.1920	20.2.1920/ 7.2.1921
30.1.1930/16.2.1931	17.2.1931/ 5.2.1932	6.2.1932/25.1.1933
15.2.1942/ 4.2.1943	5.2.1943/24.1.1944	25.1.1944/12.2.1945
3.2.1954/23.1.1955	24.1.1955/11.2.1956	12.2.1956/30.1.1957
21.1.1966/ 8.2.1967	9.2.1967/28.1.1968	29.1.1968/16.2.1969
7.2.1978/27.1.1979	28.1.1979/15.2.1980	16.2.1980/ 4.2.1981
27.1.1990/14.2.1991	15.2.1991/ 3.2.1992	4.2.1992/22.1.1993

THE ROOSTER	THE DOG	THE PIG
22.1.1909/ 9.2.1910	10.2.1910/29.1.1911	30.1.1911/17.2.1912
8.2.1921/27.1.1922	28.1.1922/15.2.1923	16.2.1923/ 4.2.1924
26.1.1933/13.2.1934	14.2.1934/ 3.2.1935	4.2.1935/23.1.1936
13.2.1945/ 1.2.1946	2.2.1946/21.1.1947	22.1.1947/ 9.2.1948
31.1.1957/15.2.1958	16.2.1958/ 7.2.1959	8.2.1959/27.1.1960
17.2.1969/ 5.2.1970	6.2.1970/26.1.1971	27.1.1971/14.2.1972
5.2.1981/24.1.1982	25.1.1982/12.2.1983	13.2.1983/ 1.2.1984
23.1.1993/ 9.2.1994	10.2.1994/30.1.1995	31.1.1995/18.2.1996

*The dates indicated specify the **first** and the **last** day of the year of the sign.*

THE HANDBOOK OF CHINESE HOROSCOPES

Theodora Lau

Are you a sentimental but crafty Rat, a serious and dutiful Ox, or a capitivating but unpredictable Tiger? Here, in the most comprehensive book ever written on Chinese astrology, you can find out which of the twelve animal signs of the lunar calendar is yours, how your sign is affected by the Yin and Yang, how your Moon sign and your Sun sign affect each other — and which of the other animal signs you're compatible with.

THE BOOK OF CHINESE BELIEFS

Frena Bloomfield

Earth magic, ghost weddings, passports to the after-life, the spirit world of the Chinese exists side-by-side with everyday reality, and affects every aspect of Chinese life from diet and decor to getting married or opening a business.

Frena Bloomfield has lived and worked in Hong Kong and has talked in depth to many practitioners of the magic arts. THE BOOK OF CHINESE BELIEFS is a fascinating introduction to a rich culture where the dead are ever-present and even the siting of a house or village is governed by the laws of earth magic.

HOROSCOPES

Arrow publish an individual Super Horoscope book for each of the twelve signs of the Zodiac, and the definitive *Handbook of Chinese Horoscopes* by Theodora Lau. These books can be bought in your local bookshop or you can order these directly by completing the form below.

SUPER HOROSCOPES 1984

____ ARIES (21 March – 20 April)	£1.50
____ TAURUS (21 April – 20 May)	£1.50
____ GEMINI (21 May – 20 June)	£1.50
____ CANCER (21 June – 20 July)	£1.50
____ LEO (21 July – 20 August)	£1.50
____ VIRGO (22 August – 22 September)	£1.50
____ LIBRA (23 September – 22 October)	£1.50
____ SCORPIO (23 October – 22 November)	£1.50
____ SAGITTARIUS (23 November – 20 December)	£1.50
____ CAPRICORN (21 December – 19 January)	£1.50
____ AQUARIUS (20 January – 18 February)	£1.50
____ PISCES (19 February – 20 March)	£1.50

Also available

____ HANDBOOK OF CHINESE HOROSCOPES	£1.95
Postage	_____
Total	_____

ARROW BOOKS, BOOKSERVICE BY POST, PO BOX 29, DOUGLAS, ISLE OF MAN

Please enclose a cheque or postal order made out to Arrow Books Limited for the amount due including 10p per book for postage and packing within the UK and 12p for overseas orders.

Please print clearly

NAME ....

ADDRESS ....

....

Whilst every effort is made to keep prices down and to keep popular books in print, Arrow Books cannot guarantee that prices will be the same as those advertised here or that books will be available.